Excellent analyses about schools that have forged their own paths to growth and renewal. The authors have researched diverse Lutheran schools around the world. From that research, ideas and thoughts about leadership, learning, and sharing the Gospel have emerged. The lessons that can be learned are meaningful to anyone who is interested in educational success or even leadership in general.

Deborah Carter, PhD, Assistant Professor,
Concordia College—New York

Imagine the Possibilities is like a delicious cake slathered with frosting—except you eat the frosting first. Indulging in the eleven case studies feeds the passion for sustaining Lutheran schools into the future. The cake comes at the end, with twenty-five neatly organized layers of lessons to learn from the featured schools. The one danger is that only administrators will read this book, when it really needs to be in the eyes, minds, and hearts of pastors, board members, and other school leaders.

Edward Grube, LLD, Director of Publications &
Communications, Lutheran Education Association

This is necessary reading for every student who aspires to serve in Lutheran schools and for the faculty who teach them. Authors Bull and Pingel skillfully help readers "imagine the breadth of possibilities for Lutheran education, considering the affordances and limitations of each" (p. 178). The work inspires readers to consider current and future possibilities for Lutheran education by telling the compelling stories of eleven mission-centered, Christ-focused Lutheran schools.

The final chapter's "twenty-five lessons learned" alone are worth the price of the book and are a rich resource for Lutheran school and congregational leaders who desire to rethink, refocus, and reenergize the mission and vision of their Lutheran schools.

Well done, Drs. Bull and Pingel! Thank you for reminding us that Lutheran education, by God's grace, continues to thrive in depth and breadth and remains God's tool of Gospel proclamation.

Rev. Brian L. Friedrich, PhD, President,
Concordia University Nebraska

D1563158

Imagine the Possibilities tells the stories of eleven diverse Lutheran schools, yet one story of a shared mission. It is vocation carried out on an international scale as, collectively, Lutheran schools mimic the apostle Paul's desire to be all things to all people for the sake of the Gospel.

This is not a book of solutions. Or, at least, it's not about a solution scripted for your school. Bull and Pingel celebrate how particular Lutheran communities have arrived at solutions specific to their local context. They offer these eleven stories as inspiration and encouragement for other schools to take their faith identity seriously. There is no one way to do Lutheran education right. *Imagine the Possibilities* demonstrates how a commitment to the best models of education, when driven by a mission to share the Gospel, empowers Lutheran schools to serve both the academic and spiritual needs of the students entrusted to their care.

Tim Schumacher, MA, Assistant Professor,
Concordia University, Irvine

I enjoyed the challenge the authors shared with us in the middle of the book: "Scripture does not offer us a single, prescribed way for doing Lutheran education in the twenty-first century" (p. 147). AMEN! This book gives us glimpses of several very different Lutheran schools that are thriving in a variety of settings as each embraces its own unique approach to education. After reading these stories, you can't help but be excited to start the conversation about how God can use your school to have an even greater impact on the families He has called you to serve.

Travis Grulke, MA, Assistant to the President—
Superintendent of Schools, Michigan District, LCMS

Pingel and Bull have provided a valuable service to Lutheran schools and the entire Christian community as they showcase a variety of educational approaches that encourage stakeholders in Christian education to imagine the possibilities. From schools that struggle financially in urban and changing communities, to a rural three-room school, to schools that have become a school of choice in wealthy neighborhoods, we see how

Lutheran schools are adapting to new settings and challenges while maintaining their Lutheran identity. This is a must-read for all who desire to make Christian education meaningful in the context God has given them.

Becky Peters, EdD, Director of Lutheran Teaching Ministry,
Concordia University, Irvine, and CPH author of
Building Faith One Child at a Time

The future of Lutheran education is strong, as evidenced by the powerful stories of Bull and Pingel. As change has come to the world through the technological revolution of the twenty-first century, so has change come to Lutheran education. Powerful storytelling throughout the book provides a glimpse of God's handiwork alive in the schools. Each story should provide hope for educators and administrators of any school. Technology, imagination, faith, and critical problem solving have provided paths for Lutheran education to be successful in nearly all corners of the world!

Jake Hollatz, EdD, Principal, St. John's Lutheran School,
Orange, CA, and CPH author of Faithfully Connected

Imagination can be a source of anxiety and fear or, with the Spirit's enlightening, the embryo of creativity and possibility. These authors have opted for the latter and open up to Christian educators a world of strategic options. Their scholarly backgrounds lead them to more than random sampling, but instead to considered examples of excellence. Bull and Pingel resist the temptation to pedagogical partisanship or ideological narrowness and offer diverse applications for those who love Christ and His children. Here, there are a variety of ways to be both flexible in your context and faithful to your core mission.

Rev. John Nunes, PhD, President,
Concordia College—New York

IMAGINE THE POSSIBILITIES

Conversations on the Future of CHRISTIAN EDUCATION

Bernard Bull • Jim Pingel

CONCORDIA PUBLISHING HOUSE • SAINT LOUIS

Published by Concordia Publishing House
3558 S. Jefferson Ave., St. Louis, MO 63118-3968
1-800-325-3040 • cph.org

Manufactured in the United States of America

Library of Congress Cataloging-in-Publication Data

Names: Pingel, James, author. | Bull, Bernard Dean, author.

Title: Imagine the possibilities : conversations on the future of Christian

　　　education / by Dr. James Pingel and Dr. Bernard Bull.

Description: Saint Louis : Concordia Publishing House, 2018.

Identifiers: LCCN 2018018892 (print) | LCCN 2018032902 (ebook) | ISBN

　　　9780758659309　| ISBN 9780758659293 (alk. paper)

Subjects: LCSH: Lutheran Church--United States--Education. | Church and

　　　education--United States.

Classification: LCC LC574 (ebook) | LCC LC574 .P56 2018 (print) | DDC

　　　371.071/41--dc23

LC record available at https://lccn.loc.gov/2018018892

2 3 4 5 6 7 8 9 10　　　　　　　27 26 25 24 23 22 21 20 19

*To all Lutheran school administrators who never dreamed
of becoming one,*

*to all Lutheran teachers and support staff whose bonus checks
are yet to come,*

*and to all future Lutheran educators and administrators who will dare
to be countercultural
while serving and teaching God's Word and Jesus.*

ACKNOWLEDGMENTS

Without the input from administrators, faculty, and staff of the schools we featured, this book could not have been completed. We sincerely appreciate their willingness to give insights about their school and programs amid all their personal and professional busyness. The interviews conducted in person, online, and through their writing not only provided us an insider's perspective of their school or programs but also inspired us with their passion for ministry, students, and families. In addition to helping us complete the project, we got to meet some wonderfully talented and dedicated colleagues in Christ.

At Our Savior Evangelical Lutheran Church and School, we thank Deaconess Sara Bielby and Rev. Christopher I. Thoma. Their demonstration of a positive and integrated church and school partnership is a model and inspiration for Lutheran schools.

At Holy Cross Lutheran School and Church, we are grateful for the time and input provided by Sherri Mackey, Soraya Trujillo, Pastor Dennis Bartels, Beverly Thompson, Sam Ludington, and Mark Brink. Despite visiting the school only a few weeks after Hurricane Irma rocked southern Florida and significantly damaged the roof of their school, they still managed to provide great southern hospitality and demonstrate how they are rescuing kittens and, more importantly, souls one student at a time.

At Crean Lutheran High School, we thank Brian Underwood, Jasmine Anderson, Jacquie Antoun, Ben Fisher, Tara Mathis, Karen Worthington, Conni Schramm, Eric Olson, Daniel Moyer, Christine Cosenza, Sherrie Lah, Lauren Yakinian, Nicole Deyke, and especially Jeffrey Beavers—whose enthusiasm and hospitality were greatly appreciated.

At Amazing Grace Christian School and Renton Prep, we thank Abbey Zenk, Kayla Vrudny, Dr. Michelle Zimmerman, Lauri Nichols, Gloria Zimmerman, and Dr. David-Paul Zimmerman. Informally, the research for the chapter on these two truly amazing schools started years ago with a visit to Amazing Grace. Over the years, we've followed their work with delight. In fact, Amazing Grace is partly the inspiration for this book, offering a sense of hope for what is truly possible in Lutheran education beyond traditional models and practices.

At Immanuel Lutheran School, we thank Headmaster Julia Habrecht for her leadership and primary source of insight about the school. We also thank Rev.

Christopher Esget for his vision and leadership, as well as the many others who have contributed to this exemplary Lutheran school.

At Lutheran High School in Parker, Colorado, we give thanks for David Ness, David Black, Hannah Buchholz, and Dan Gehrke—truly one of the most innovative and grounded leaders in the entire Lutheran education system.

At the Lutheran Urban Mission Initiative (LUMIN) schools, we thank Mie Neumann, Shaun Luehring, Caroline Horn, Renate Hougard, Dennel Meinzer, Maria Wartgow, Tara Kuhl, Caroline Horn, Nicole Schmidt, Jenna Johnson, Deb Heiden, Tim Young Eagle, Cole Braun, Trila Pitchford, Trenae Howard, Cassandra Neiman, Tiffany Venegas, Sarah Weber, Julieane Cook, Jerry Krause, Kyle Jagler, and Richard Laabs—whose enthusiasm is certainly contagious.

At Concordia International School Shanghai, we thank Vivian Ton for her help coordinating everything from travel to meetings and tours. We also thank Dr. Mary Scott for her leadership, hospitality, and willingness to invite us behind the scenes of this remarkable mission in mainland China. We are also grateful for the many people who provided important insights about the school, including, but not limited to, Curt Larson, Tanya Wu, Kelly Jo Larson, Helen Hong, Genevieve Ermeling, Joel Klammer, Evelyn Chaveriat, Jane Klammer, Karin Semler, and Anne Love.

At Open Sky Education Learning Centers (with special attention to the work in St. Louis), we thank Rev. Dr. Matt Hoehner, Emily Dittmer, Andrew Neumann, Amber Kraus, Angie Molkentin, and the many others who contribute to this story of educational renewal.

At Orange Lutheran High School, we are grateful for the time and input from Todd Eklund, Patty Young, Jenny Miklos, Jill Ronstadt, Drew Heim, Kim Hahn, Rachel Eklund, Rev. Tim Detviler, Steve Barillier, and Leslie Smith, whose tenderness and tenacity are both embedded in the vision of OLu. Special thanks also to CEO Todd Moritz, who inspires so many in both his personal and professional vocations.

At Trinity Lutheran School Orchard Farm, we thank Kathryne Chapin and Esther Loeffler. Thank you for what you do and how it can inspire others to imagine the possibilities. The legacy of a Lutheran school that faithfully served families and students from the Civil War to the present is an inspiration to us all.

TABLE OF CONTENTS

Introduction

AN INVITATION TO IMAGINE THE POSSIBILITIES

And Jesus said to His disciples, "Truly, I say to you, only with difficulty will a rich person enter the kingdom of heaven. Again I tell you, it is easier for a camel to go through the eye of a needle than for a rich person to enter the kingdom of God." When the disciples heard this, they were greatly astonished, saying, "Who then can be saved?" But Jesus looked at them and said, "With man this is impossible, but with God all things are possible."

—Matthew 19:23–26

Lutheran education is alive and well. It is sometimes tempting to focus upon the stories of disappointments, failures, and closures; but those do not define the larger story of Lutheran education. Amid the tyranny of the urgent, the challenges of daily ministry in a Lutheran school, and the struggle with our own fears and sinful nature, we can and sometimes do lose sight of the incredible gift that God grants to the Christian Church and the world in the form of Lutheran schooling.

We have our challenges. The stories of closings are real and growing in some areas. Our efforts to educate with excellence sometimes fall short. Financial struggles distract, detract, and deter us. Changing demographics in communities make it confusing for us to chart a course forward. Temptations to compromise on our identity and mission in order to attract new students amid a post-Christian context are a reality in Lutheran education. With contemporary society redefining some of our fundamental beliefs as bigoted, intolerant, outdated, or sometimes even illegal, we struggle to determine the right and wise path forward. With the growth of technology and in an era of unprecedented experimentation with educational methods and philosophies, we return to the Scriptures and the seminal works of our Lutheran tradition for wisdom on when to embrace and when to reject these new developments. Even after building a robust international system of schools over the last five hundred years, we still grapple with what it means to be and function as a distinctly Lutheran school in a given time and place.

These challenges are real and important. Yet they do not define us. Our identity is in Jesus Christ. Our mission in Lutheran education comes from the Great Commission. Our future is not determined by demographics. Our struggles and doubts do not diminish God's Word. Lutheran education is alive and well because Jesus Christ is risen. As long as we are built upon the foundation of Jesus Christ, we are on firm ground. It is with this certain foundation that we approach our task in Lutheran education with courage, conviction, and confidence. We are not guaranteed every success. Enrollment numbers may ebb and flow. Detractors come and go. Social and political tensions will fluctuate. Our world is constantly changing; beliefs and values shift, displaying new expressions of humankind's persistent struggle with the realities of sin.

The wonderful news is that all of these challenges point us back to the incredible blessings and value of Lutheran education in the twenty-first century. We will continue to face challenges; some will test our resolve. God is good and faithful in those times. We lean on His promises and seek wisdom in His commands as we move forward, not by our own power, but held up by His grace and goodness.

This will look different from one context to another in contemporary Lutheran education. Missionaries respond to the contexts in which they find themselves, but their charge is to do so while testifying and holding on to the unchanging truth of God's Word, sharing the Gospel of Jesus Christ in its fullness. Lutheran schools and those who serve in them have this same honor and calling.

When we look at Lutheran education on a large scale, we see something more than these challenges. Even as some lament the closing of schools—some of which have operated for a century or more—there are just as many stories of families brought to Christ, young people nurtured in the faith, and countless students well-equipped for lives of purpose, possibility, and impact in their communities and the world.

The story of Lutheran education is not one of simple survival. It is a story of thriving, and that is the story that we want to tell in this book. *Imagine the Possibilities* grew from more than a decade of studying the state of contemporary education in the United States and beyond, starting with thousands of formal and informal interviews and hundreds of school visits and examinations of different schools. These were not just Lutheran schools. In fact, almost none of them were Lutheran schools in the first years of that exploration. Instead, this was one researcher and educator's effort simply to expand his awareness of what is happening and what is possible in modern schooling.

Growing up in Lutheran schools from age 6 all the way through my first graduate degree, when I became a university professor and administrator, I wanted to expand my knowledge about the current state of schools, especially those that were experimenting and exploring new approaches. I ventured out on what has become a lifelong journey of studying distinctive, innovative, creative, impactful, and sometimes just interesting ways to approach schooling. I learned about project-based schools, self-directed schools, place-based schools, STEM academies, experiential learning schools, classical schools, different types of international schools, national schools in different countries, schools for at-risk students, bilingual schools, art immersion schools, blended-learning schools, virtual schools, game-based-learning schools, and so much more.

The more that I learned, the more inspired I became to continue my study and exploration. I did not like or agree with everything that I saw, but I was persistently curious. At the same time, I found myself challenged to revisit many of my beliefs and values about schooling and education. I learned about countless schools with an incredible sense of compassion and community, unlike anything I had seen before. I witnessed schools where intellectual engagement and curiosity dominated the climate, and students demonstrating boredom were rare or sometimes altogether absent. I saw students thinking deeply, communicating with eloquence and conviction, taking ownership of their learning.

In short, my sense of what is possible in school expanded tenfold amid this exploration of different schools. Then, I started sharing what I saw and learned with people in Lutheran schools. I shared the good, the bad, and the ugly. I tried not to paint some utopian image of the schools. After all, we are in a fallen world, with each of us infected by sin, and that always shows itself in any human community. These schools were certainly no exception. Yet I also saw private schools that served a diverse population of students; were financially viable; had a clear, focused, and distinct approach to teaching and learning; and would be described by their community as thriving, not simply struggling to survive.

I wanted to share that with the Lutheran schooling community. I wanted to tell them about amazing classical schools that revolved around a passion for nurturing students who value truth, beauty, and goodness. I wanted people to know of project-based schools where students started social enterprises that benefited hundreds or thousands of people, all while the students were developing new content-area knowledge and thinking skills. I yearned for people to consider ways we might leverage blended and online learning to reach new students and families. I wanted Lutheran schools to know even more about the power of new and emerging research on the brain and how people are using this knowledge to increase student learning and engagement. I did not intend for people to accept or embrace every practice or approach that I shared. I certainly did not and do not. I just wanted to help people expand their sense of what is possible, to take the good and leave the rest behind, and to use this broader sense of what is possible to amplify the impact of Lutheran education in the world.

Yet I must make a confession. The more that I explored these wonderfully inspiring and lively schools, the more I found myself experiencing a growing disappointment with Lutheran schools. Why didn't I see any of this in Lutheran schools? When I went to Lutheran education conferences, why were people not aware of or at least talking about the implications of these different school models and new developments? Why did it seem like so many Lutheran schools and educators seemed to be isolated from some of the significant debates and conversations of modern education? At times, I confess to lamenting instances when it seemed like we were content surviving on mediocre education infused with a dose of Jesus.

The problem with this is that I was wrong. There are undoubtedly pockets of truth. I can find instances where my fears and thoughts are affirmed in Lutheran schools, but there are enough exceptions that it is probably not even wise for me to call them exceptions. As I started to explore further, including in Lutheran schools, I learned that there is much to learn from and celebrate in Lutheran education today.

There are many and varied Lutheran schools that are thriving; have a clear, refined, and well-supported approach to what and how they teach; have a viable financial model; and are committed not only to maintaining their Lutheran affiliation but also to allowing their Lutheran identity to persistently shape and inform what they do and how they do it. Contrary to some claims, these are not just schools in the suburbs that happen to serve families who reach the top tax brackets. These are schools serving all types of students and families. There are examples on the P–8 level and the high school level. We can find them around the United States and beyond. They also take on many and varied forms.

As I challenged and debunked my own assumptions about Lutheran education in the twenty-first century, I resolved to share this important reality with the larger Lutheran community. That is the purpose of this book. I am grateful that my friend, colleague, and fellow Lutheran educator, researcher, and leader Dr. James Pingel agreed to join me in this task. He is a keen observer, a gifted writer, and a devoted Lutheran educator and scholar. I thank God for his partnership in this project. In fact, even as I might have initiated this work based upon my larger research on models of education over the last ten or more years, he has become as much or more of a leader in making this book a reality, shaping its form and style, and making it something that I hope and believe will be a blessing to your work in Christian education. Together, we have eleven stories to share with you in this book. Each chapter is the story of a Lutheran school that is, in the view of us and others, thriving.

We only tell the stories of eleven schools in this book. There are many more stories worth telling. Yet we sought out a collection of schools and stories that helps us tell a larger story about the diversity of ways in which Lutheran education is thriving today. We selected schools from east to west, north to south. We tell the stories of schools in the heartland and venture all the way to the West Coast. We even included a story from Shanghai, China, to add an international perspective to the collection. We tell stories from Florida, Colorado, Wisconsin, Virginia, Washington, Michigan, California, and Missouri.

We share true tales of widely different approaches to education—even one that is not defined as a Lutheran school at all. There are schools that serve populations dominated by children who are eligible for free and reduced lunch. There is a school where the majority of students have their eyes set on the top universities in the world, and it is commonplace for students to achieve such a goal. There is also great diversity in the demographic and ethnic background of students served in these schools. We chose such a wide range to tell the larger story of Lutheran education—that it is thriving and in different ways.

Lutheran education is reaching and serving people from all types of backgrounds and in many contexts and communities. By sharing these stories, we hope to inspire you, the reader, for your own context and community.

These stories are not recipes for success. Each context for ministry and running a Lutheran school is distinct and constantly being reconsidered. By the time this book goes to print and you finally hold it in your hand, it's likely that some of these very schools may well have changed some of the particulars of their situations. As such, our stories are really more inspirational than replicable. They are a snapshot in time of these schools, a static portrait of schools that are anything but static, schools that are continually recalibrating in response to the many and various needs of their unique settings. You will find many suggestions and ideas that can and will work in your context, but it is certainly not as easy as repeating what another school did and expecting the same result. Instead, consider these as stories to expand your awareness, give you some good ideas to test and consider, and inspire you to create your own compelling story of a thriving Lutheran school.

Along the way, you will undoubtedly read stories and parts of stories that clash with your own beliefs and values about education in general or Lutheran education in particular. We welcome and encourage that. Read and analyze with a critical eye and with the Scriptures nearby. Just as the Bereans tested Paul's preaching with the Scriptures, we hope and pray that you will do the same. At the same time, we invite you to approach your reading with enough openness to at least imagine the broader possibilities. You can and should critique and analyze, but also challenge your own assumptions. This is, after all, a wonderfully Lutheran way to approach education and learning. We learn with intellectual humility, recognizing our flaws, sins, and limitations, and therefore being willing to listen and learn from others, even from often diverse and divergent viewpoints. You will find some of those in the pages of this book. So read with humility but also with your Bible nearby: testing, pondering, challenging, and learning.

We hope and pray that by the time you finish this book your sense of what is possible will be expanded, you are inspired to deepen the impact and vitality of Lutheran schools, you have a renewed sense of pride in our Lutheran education system, your appreciation of Lutheran education as an incredible gift and resource in the church will have grown, and you are inspired to embark on your own effort to create or tell a future story of a thriving Lutheran school.

As you read these eleven stories, there is a simple pattern to each story. Knowing that pattern in advance may help you to follow along. Each story illustrates a challenge faced by a school or a promising opportunity that people pursued in a given school; we start each story with a summary of that challenge or opportunity. Following that short introduction, we tell you the story: What was the background? How did it come about? What were some critical elements of that story? Third, we report on some of the goals and desired outcomes associated with whatever challenge or opportunity the school pursued. Fourth, we share some of the results. Some stories have clearer conclusions and more measurable results than others, but all of the stories include insight into how things went or are going. Finally, we conclude each chapter with a few lessons learned. Sometimes these lessons were learned by the people at the school. In other cases, this section infuses a few reflections and lessons from the author of that chapter.

After you finish the final story, we have a concluding chapter where we pull together twenty-five lessons learned from the different stories in the book. These are candid lessons and reflections from the two authors, and we offer them for your prayerful consideration. Even more important, we hope that you will document your own lessons learned as you work your way through this book and as you seek to use what you learn to further the mission and ministry of Lutheran education.

Before I finish this introductory chapter, I want to offer our wholehearted thanks to you as the reader. Dr. Pingel and I both realize that there are countless education books available today and that we all have busy lives. It is humbling for us to know that you consider this book to be worth some of that time. As such, we pray that the stories and insights in this book are well worth your time and that you will be encouraged, challenged, inspired, and further equipped to continue your good and important work in Christian education and beyond.

Together in His Service,
Dr. Bernard Bull

"Free, Family, and Faith Formation"

THE TUITION-FREE LUTHERAN SCHOOL:

OUR SAVIOR EVANGELICAL LUTHERAN CHURCH AND SCHOOL

HARTLAND, MI

The Challenge and Opportunity: Declining Enrollment and a New Vision

When it comes to the community at Our Savior Evangelical Lutheran Church and School, the pastor has a saying that embodies much of what they do: "All roads lead to the nave." This is the place where people gather around Word and Sacrament, and the nave also represents the fact that this is indeed the center of mission and ministry for both the church and school. This close connection between church and school and the pastor's passionate pursuit of practices that draw the community close to God's Word are also at the heart of one of this school's most distinct traits: it is tuition-free for members and nonmembers alike, and that money comes from the cheerful support of the church.

THE OUR SAVIOR EVANGELICAL LUTHERAN SCHOOL STORY

The story of Our Savior Evangelical Lutheran School goes back almost forty years, when the school was first founded, but our story begins in more recent times, around 2007. At that point, an individual who had served at the church in different capacities was ordained and became the sole pastor. Over the years, the congregation went through times of financial struggle before the school was tuition-free. As the pastor describes it, they were a parochial school in the most traditional and literal sense. Following a practice common in some congregation schools of the past, member families sending their children to the school paid no tuition, and nonmember families sending their children to the school paid tuition, but the tuition did not make a significant impact on the school budget. At this stage, the school had any number of options. They could switch to tuition for all students. They could raise tuition for nonmembers. They could disinvest in the school part of the ministry altogether. Yet they considered an altogether different option. The pastor mused, How do we become the only game in town, stand out, get confessional Lutheran education out in front of other people? As he crunched the numbers, considered the challenges and implications of dwindling enrollment, and realized that their tuition-dependent model did not cover the costs anyway, he looked to God's Word for direction.

Committed to founding everything that the church does upon the Scriptures and Lutheran Confessions, he reflected on Paul's ministry. The pastor asked himself, Did Paul charge tuition to nonmembers who wanted to hear the preaching of the Gospel? If not, then maybe Our Savior should consider a similar model. Amid such prayerful reflection, he started a conversation about a bold and rare way forward: to turn Our Savior into a tuition-free confessional Lutheran school for all students who attend, member and nonmember alike.

While this might look like a purely financial decision, the results were far more than financial. First, this was not just about making the school tuition-free. This was a charge to the congregation to think deeply about stewardship, vision, and a focused direction. It can be hard for members of the congregation to get behind something intangible, but this specific and tangible vision of a Gospel-inspired tuition-free school was something specific and compelling. While members of the congregation had long supported the idea of the day school, even seeing it as a main mission of the church, people were not necessarily behind it financially. With this decision, that changed in some amazing ways.

In fact, the stewardship trend at the church changed significantly. As people began to discuss and more clearly understand how the school fit into the church mission, financial giving increased as well. Giving-percentage groups shifted. The group of members who previously gave in the range of 1–2 percent of their income now jumped to giving 5–6 percent. The pastor recalled how, at a prayer vigil, a member disclosed that he had not given as he could have in the past, but he was delighted with the school shift and wanted to see it flourish in ways never seen before; this man gave financially to the cause and continues to be an ongoing partner in this ministry. This is one of many examples of church members who, over time, became strong supporters and deeply engaged in the mission of the school.

In addition, both the pastor and school principal can tell many stories of giving and financial support from members, nonmembers, and members who do not have children attending the school. Even amid struggles, nonmembers are giving large gifts to the church, earmarked for the school. They are giving because they are thankful. When real needs are shared, people step up and help out financially. In addition, there are members of the congregation who do have not direct ties to the school by children or grandchildren benefiting from the education, but some of these people are still among the more generous givers to the mission.

It is not just about giving either. It is also about how this decision contributed to the formation of a growing family and community environment. Becoming tuition-free shifted the way that people approach and think about this school. The pastor and principal described how, in the past, tuition-paying families sometimes approached school as a product or service, with the mindset of a customer. As the pastor explained, "In many other schools, there is a consumer-driven mind-set with tuition. In this school, it doesn't work quite that way. That consumer mindset has evaporated in the school and congregation, as has the separation of church and school families." In the words of the pastor, "Now the church has the muscle to actually be the church and to better assimilate the people we serve into our identity."

This family environment is even evident in the way that parents support one another and approach discipline issues and other life challenges. When one child is wronged by another child, it is not consistently about parents being eager to defend their own child. In fact, the principal reported parents also showing concern for the other child. When a boy in a nonmember family lost his father, there was a great showing of members who attended the funeral.

This community of engagement is a truly distinct element of the school. Having moved away from that consumer model, there is much more of a volunteer and support mind-set. The Parent Teacher League is a valuable part of that. While there is not tuition, there is a point system where each parent agrees to contribute to the community in various ways, often through volunteer assistance. Yet, even apart from this, there is a strong culture of volunteering. One parent started and runs an after-school Lego robotics team. A church member with no family attending the school volunteers and runs a chess team after school. At Christmas, there is a Christmas giving tree, providing member and nonmember families an opportunity to give something to the school as a Christmas present. The principal reported just short of $1,000 in gifts received as Christmas presents in 2017.

As already mentioned, "all roads lead to the nave" in this community, and to reinforce this fact, every new school week begins there. The entire school community gathers in the nave right away on Monday morning, centered around prayer in the Order of Matins. The pastor shares, "We meet again on Thursday mornings and use the Order of Responsive Prayer with a focus on liturgics, which is the opportunity to not only be fed by God's Word but to do so through intentional catechesis with regard to why we do what we do as Christians in worship." Why do we gather in the nave each Monday morning? Why is there an altar? Why are we gathering? Then, as students and teachers go to their classes, they take what they learned in the nave with them. From the classroom, they carry these messages from the nave back to their families as well.

Connected to this bold tuition-free decision, the preadmission and admission process has changed. Leadership explains that when families come for a school tour, they are not trying to sell the school as much as communicate the school's distinct confessional Lutheran identity. They explain that they will take church attendance, not to police families, but because this school wants to partner in raising children in the faith. They are clear that Lutheran doctrine will be taught and that they will be asking children to sing in Sunday worship once a month, contributing to the service through their gift of song. The goal is to be as clear and candid as possible so that parents can make a wise and informed decision about whether they want to be part of such an intentional and immersive community.

In general, the families drawn to such a school are members of the church or of another Christian church, with about a 60/40 split between children from member and nonmember congregations. This is a significant change from the time before free tuition, when enrollment was only about 20 percent non-member families. Families that long for a Christian education but have three or more children and would struggle to afford it elsewhere can find a home at Our Savior.

Unlike other schools with a tuition-dependent model, Our Savior is not driven to continual and larger enrollment sizes. They have a realistic cap for each class. They want to keep class sizes reasonable, and they also recognize that they do not have the resources to serve students with certain special needs. There is an interview process, and while the leader communicates a vision for a largely welcome and open community, they also have to consider with each new applicant what is best for the family and the entire school community. They do not take the denial of enrollment lightly, nor do they use this in some effort to curate an elite academic climate. They are far more concerned with nurturing the family and the larger community. With current support from the congregation and the existing staffing needs, they are equipped to serve up to one hundred students. If they want to grow beyond that, they will do so prayerfully and carefully, considering whether they have the resources to do that well, to serve and support the community with excellence.

While the tuition-free model is perhaps one of the most striking distinctions of this school, it is not the only one. Other distinctions include curricular decisions and a fascinating experiment intended to improve the social climate in the school.

The school's constant pursuit of practices that draw them back to the Lutheran Confessions and the Scriptures informs their ongoing approach to curriculum. At the time of the interview with school leaders, they were at the early stages of exploring a move toward becoming a classical school, resonating with the focus on absolute truth in such a curriculum. As with many things at the school, they are not making hurried decisions. They are prayerful and deliberate, taking time to learn through reading books on the subject together, attending the Consortium of Classical Lutheran Education conference, visiting another classical school, and finding people with whom they can ask and explore their questions. The school is also a thoughtful critic of what they would identify as "serious deficiencies—both philosophically and pedagogically—that shape the underlying beliefs and values associated with the

Common Core State Standards, and this stance is something that draws the interest of the families who choose to send their children to the school." There is clearly an appreciation for the school's commitment to evaluating external standards and school practices through the lens of a distinctly Lutheran theology and philosophy of education.

Amid concern over a couple of behavioral issues in the school and explorations of a more classical model of education, the school also moved to a house model, which started to take shape in 2016. Each class has an assignment to one of two houses: Luther House or Walther House. When it first started, it didn't take off. Yet, as they have become more intentional about the house system, it has since become a growing part of the community. The leadership reports this model creating community and healthy competition among students, often in the form of things like a collection competition at Thanksgiving and Christmas. Houses compete throughout the year on such things, with one house winning the challenge for the year.

GOALS AND DESIRED OUTCOMES

More than anything else, the goal of the many efforts described in this chapter brings us back to the persistent pursuit of discovering what it means to have a church and school mission that is shaped and informed by the Lutheran Confessions and the Scriptures. Inspired by Paul's sharing of the Gospel free of charge, the school sought to do the same with its mission. This also allowed the school to differentiate itself from the various private, Lutheran, and other school options for families in the community. In doing so, Our Savior moved beyond the idea of competing with other schools for students, instead discovering a financially viable model that was inspired by their study of the Scriptures, made the school a central mission of the church, and met a truly distinct need for families in the community.

RESULTS AND OUTCOMES

As outlined in the previous pages, the decision to become tuition free and the work that went into the congregation embracing that approach is producing a number of benefits. The school managed to shift the parent mind-set from consumer to community member. The division between member and nonmember families diminished or disappeared. The entire church and community support for and engagement in the school deepened. School enrollment rebounded from past times. Amid all of this, the school is a clear and distinct option for families in the community that want an intentionally Christian education.

LESSONS FROM OUR SAVIOR EVANGELICAL LUTHERAN SCHOOL

Decisions about how to function as a Lutheran school are deeply contextual. Schools must respond to their unique time and location. Yet there are unchanging truths that can and should shape what Lutheran schools do as well. We see both of these at work in a school like Our Savior. Beyond that, consider these additional lessons from this school.

The Power of Community

At first, the story seems to be about the impressive shift to a tuition-free model, but the closer one looks, the more apparent it is that the headliner is their tremendous community. The decision about tuition assisted with this, but behind that decision is a grand story about creating a shared vision, lots of conversation, and countless intentional efforts to build a certain type of Christian community.

Moving beyond the Consumer Mind-Set

This notion of helping parents think about the school community as members more than as consumers is a compelling consideration for Lutheran schools. While not all schools will find the tuition-free model achievable, it is still worthwhile to consider other practices to help shift thinking from consumer to the primary role of a valued, active, and engaged member of an interdependent community.

All Roads Lead to the Nave

This phrase is repeated throughout the chapter because it is repeated often in the church and school. There are two things to note about this. One is the powerful concept, which can help people see important relationships and priorities in the school. Another lesson is simply the idea of creating short statements that are packed with meaning and used to build a shared understanding of the community's identity and orientation.

The Blessing of a Strong Church/School Dynamic

Many Lutheran schools celebrate a strong and healthy partnership between the church and school, but this is an especially strong example. The pastor and principal work closely with each other, supporting each other and honoring distinct roles, but there is something particularly noteworthy in this case. At the time of writing this chapter, the principal is a trained deaconess who also has significant experience in project management from the business world. As a deaconess, the principal's education and experience included working alongside the pastor. The result is a wonderfully dynamic relationship where each distinct role is honored and unique gifts are combined for the good of the school and community as they work together toward a shared vision. This is clearly a dynamic that strengthens the church-school relationship. Furthermore, the pastor chooses to view the school as a primary mission of the church and takes the initiative to help build a shared vision around that view in the congregation. This shared approach to the school mission is certainly a good starting point for such a strong and positive church-school dynamic. In fact, I intentionally avoided the word *partnership* when writing about the church-school relationship because this example is not two entities coming together. The school is a mission of the church. It is already an integrated part of the church. It is just a matter of making that relationship a healthy and positive one.

School as a Mission of the Church

While just stated in the last lesson, this is significant enough to warrant its own designation. This is a model where the school is indeed seen as a mission, even a primary mission, of the congregation. It is not a separate entity. This is not true for other Lutheran schools. Some keep the budgets, boards, and many other aspects completely separate. Some even argue for greater independence and autonomy. Without making a judgment about these other approaches, the model in this chapter demonstrates a different way forward.

Let the Mission Inform Policies and Practices

Notice that, in this story, the Scriptures played a central role in shaping the pastor's thinking about tuition. Some do not think of finances and other business functions as opportunities to live out the mission, to embody a commitment to the Scriptures. Yet, this school's approach demonstrates how that can and does happen and shows some of the wonderful blessings that come from taking the time and care to do so.

Building Consensus

The decision to go tuition-free is not easy, nor is the choice to become a classical Lutheran school. Yet leadership is committed to taking the time to discuss, study together, and help the congregation develop an important understanding of such matters. There is great attention to the why behind the how, and that is an opportunity to deepen the congregation's commitment to its core mission.

The Importance of a Leader with Vision

The pastor of the congregation is a key visionary in the church and the school as a mission. No small number of ideas shared in this chapter started with his prayerful consideration. The principal plays a key role in setting vision in certain areas as well. In all the schools outlined in this book and those studied over the years, this is a constant trait of high-impact and distinct organizations. We are wise not to underestimate the importance of leaders with vision.

Differentiation over Competition

Another thought-provoking lesson in this particular case was the reflection about how a school can distinguish itself in the community. Instead of just engaging in a direct competition with the other schools in the area, Our Savior opted to find out what their school is uniquely positioned to do that could be a blessing to families. That differentiation versus competition mind-set is potentially useful in many Lutheran school contexts. Yet part of what makes this so compelling is that the desire to differentiate was not the primary reason for being tuition-free. Rather, it started with a Gospel motivation, inspired by an Early Church model of Paul freely sharing the Gospel without charge.

The Ripple Effect

It is hard to deny the ripple effect of going tuition-free. It has a massive impact on many things in the school, even contributing to a full culture and climate shift. We cannot always predict the consequences and results of policy and practice changes, but it is critical for leaders navigating change in Lutheran education to recognize that a ripple effect exists and is common with large decisions.

Concluding Thoughts

Throughout this text, there are multiple financial models for Lutheran schools—everything from tuition-dependence to government funding to this much rarer but intriguing tuition-free option. It might not be achievable or desirable in every context, but it nonetheless gives us all a chance to pause and consider that there are many ways to fund a Lutheran school and important implications for whichever funding we select.

"Bloom Where You Are Planted"

2

The Challenge and Opportunity: Ministry in a Community with Significant Demographic Change

Cars and vans carefully approach the drop-off point in front of the school. Several teachers and administrators, holding umbrellas on this rainy day in North Miami, Florida, welcome the students and their families with high fives, hugs, and friendly banter. Most of the faces are happy and joy-filled, except for a few kids who are concerned about a kitten—which somehow avoided getting run over by an SUV and worked its way into the engine block of the vehicle. After several minutes of investigative work underneath the SUV and with the help of Assistant Principal Soraya Trujillo, the kitten is located and rescued. Shaking profusely because it is cold, scared, or injured, the rescued kitten is brought into the school office and placed in a box filled with blankets. Concerned students hope the hastily arranged, makeshift shelter will provide the needed respite and recovery for their new feline friend. "This whole scene is just like the Holy Cross family," someone says. "We welcome them in no matter where we find them and no matter what shape they are in."

Holy Cross Lutheran School is in North Miami, the urban fringe of Miami. Over four hundred students attend the school, starting from age 2 all the way through eighth grade. The student body mirrors the ethnicity and demographic of their particular neighborhood, which is mostly composed of working-class Afro-Caribbean people, primarily Haitian Americans. The community has undergone significant demographic change in the last three decades and remains transient today. Holy Cross Lutheran Church, connected and directly affiliated with the school, sees 25–30 percent of its membership turn over each year. Most of the teachers at Holy Cross are Protestant, and a few are Lutheran. Their salary is approximately 30 percent less than their public school counterparts.

Even though tuition is about $7,000 per student, few families actually pay anywhere close to the sticker price. While most contribute or pay at least some tuition, about 75 percent of families receive some kind of financial aid or financial assistance. In addition, due to Title I funding, all students are eligible for a free breakfast and lunch.

Holy Cross is largely funded through the Step Up for Students scholarship program—Florida's largest school voucher program—designed so that private corporations and donors can make contributions to an independent trust fund in lieu of paying a percentage of taxes on their capital gains. Qualifying families receive need-based scholarships or vouchers, which can be used at parochial schools. Families, of course, are responsible for paying any difference between the voucher amount and a school's tuition. Created to benefit children whose educational options are limited by household income, Step Up for Student's scholarships are not tied to the performance of public schools nor to the performance of students who receive them. Due to the longevity and notable success of the nonprofit funding organization, Holy Cross administrators are not worried that the Step Up for Students program might be eliminated due to pressure from public teacher unions, lobbyists, or those who oppose private or parochial education. Despite Holy Cross's reputation for being a safe, academically excellent Christian school, there is no doubt that without Florida's voucher system, the school's enrollment would be significantly less.

As the gateway to Latin America and the Caribbean, Miami is made up of two different worlds—one where wealthy families and their fortunes remain wrapped up in land acquisition, trade, and tourism, and one where the working class struggles with the high costs of food, housing, rent, and insurance. Families that struggle to make ends meet are the ones that Holy Cross serves and ministers to daily.

As Holy Cross ministers to the underserved, there is no shortage of love, care, and dedication in preparing these young children for the future. Every morning, students and faculty gather in one of the open courtyards on campus. First, they recite the Pledge of Allegiance to the US flag, followed by the pledge to the Christian cross. Then, students and staff belt out the song "God Bless America." Finally, they end the morning muster by speaking the Lord's Prayer. With students dressed in uniforms and wearing the same school colors, the scene is patriotic, touching, unifying, and faith-affirming.

From the very first moment of the day, students experience how the administration, faculty, and staff keep the love of Christ at the forefront of their mission. Holy Cross personifies the ministry of tomorrow, embracing the different cultures and backgrounds of their students all for the sake of sharing and teaching the Gospel. While the neighborhood demographics have shifted over the years in North Miami, one thing that has not changed at Holy Cross Lutheran School is teaching and sharing the love of Christ.

However, over the last two decades in particular, Holy Cross leaders have adjusted their curriculum and changed their outreach approach in a culturally sensitive manner. Rather than expecting people with different cultures and ethnic backgrounds to change for them, the leadership of Holy Cross reflected on and brainstormed different ways they could reach out and adapt to the demographic changes that swept over North Miami like a tidal wave. Every administrator, faculty, and staff member insists that their approach to ministry is simple: ministry is not about connecting to a *culture* as much as it is about connecting to *people*. No matter the cultural or ethnic background, every single person is a child of God, and every child of God should know that he or she is loved, forgiven, and redeemed thanks to the blood of Jesus Christ. "We as a church have not done a good job of going and making disciples of all nations," Holy Cross Pastor Dennis Bartels insists. "The Lord has placed Holy Cross in a location where nations have come to us, and we need to be ready to serve." He adds: "The Message never changes, so we work hard at making sure the love of Jesus is shared in as many ways as we can while still being true to His Word."

ADJUSTING TO AND EMBRACING SIGNIFICANT DEMOGRAPHIC CHANGE

Holy Cross Lutheran Church and School have been educating and serving the greater Miami community since 1951. The ministry began in one building with the kindergarten program, serving eight to ten students in its first few years. On Saturdays, school and congregation members would physically transform the kindergarten classroom into a worship center. School materials and desks were moved out onto the porch of the building while all the chairs and other needed items were put into place for the Sunday morning worship service. Then on Sunday afternoon, volunteers would reconvert the building into the kindergarten room so that school could commence without interruption on Monday morning. New grade levels were added each year. The school expanded—both in numbers and in the size of its campus. A healthy and vibrant church-school partnership still exists and is evident sixty-six years later.

The story gets especially interesting in the 1990s, when a great number of white, middle-class families left Dade County (where Holy Cross is located) and moved north to Broward County. In 1993, 95 percent of the Holy Cross Lutheran School student body was white. As white flight took place throughout the remainder of the 1990s, many different Afro-Caribbean, Hispanic, Latino, and black families moved and settled in the North Miami region.

The huge demographic shift in the 1990s compelled Holy Cross to make a pivotal decision. Instead of leaving the community as so many other organizations and private schools did, Holy Cross Lutheran School would stay in the community and embrace a "bloom where you are planted" vision of ministry. In fact, by the late 1990s, Holy Cross had 220 students with 47 different countries and nationalities represented among its student body. A decade later in 2004, about 50 percent of students were white and 50 percent multiethnic. The changing demographics continued throughout the next decade and a half in the twenty-first century. Today, the school is almost 98 percent black, mostly Haitian. Says one Holy Cross school official, "I make no pretense about this, but our school community is like much of Haiti is today. We face many of the same challenges third-world countries do right here in south Florida."

The administration, faculty, and staff of Holy Cross have experienced transformation throughout the years too. The current faculty more closely resembles the demographics of the student body, which sends an important message and provides a level of identity comfort to prospective families. "I want to believe our school and church is what heaven looks like," asserts one teacher. Moreover, engagement and learning often increase when students are taught by teachers who look like them.

Not only has the faculty and administration diversified over the years but so have some of the attributes and characteristics Principal Sherri Mackey looks for in potential teacher candidates. Mackey is a second-career school leader with a background in business and marketing. Before she became principal of Holy Cross Lutheran School, she worked in advertising for the *Miami Herald*. Mackey, who has faithfully served the school for almost three decades, believes her second-career background has actually been a blessing and advantage for her, especially considering the demographic change that has occurred in the community and at Holy Cross. According to Mackey, second-career professionals have a different outlook on things. They do not get distracted by petty details but stay focused on the essentials. They are less worried about their own egos and hurting people's feelings and more focused on results and mission fruition. Moreover, second-career professionals are not attached to a specific process, strategy, or ideology. Instead, they employ whatever method or approach is needed to get the job done. For Mackey, second-career people adjust to change quicker, see change coming faster, and are not afraid to switch approaches or pedagogy when necessary. In addition to her experience in dealing with second-career professionals and leaders, she notes it takes a special person to teach in the urban fringe of Miami. Mackey makes it clear that when there are teacher openings at Holy Cross, she looks for traditionally trained LCMS church workers as well as second-career professionals. "Both types have their virtues and struggles," she says. "Unfortunately, we've invested in so many teachers over the years who come from areas outside of Florida or don't have an urban background only to have them leave after a short time here," she laments. "When I look for people now, I look for Christ-centered teachers who want to be in an urban setting and want to invest in south Florida. It's only fair to them and to us."

To a person, the one individual who gets credit and accolades for leading the mission and ministry of Holy Cross Lutheran School, especially during the last few decades of momentous demographic change, is Pastor Bartels. "We would not be where we are today as a school," insists Mackey, "without a pastor who was humble, flexible, and able to adapt to changing community trends and who empowered us (faculty and staff) to carry out this vision." In fact, Pastor Bartel's humility inspired Mackey to become a Lutheran and officially join Holy Cross Lutheran Church. "The same man you see every day at the school, tirelessly working to serve others, is the same man you see in the pulpit," she asserts. "He walks the talk." Many faculty and staff members who are not Lutheran frequently attend worship services at Holy Cross due mainly to their admiration and respect for Pastor Bartels. Having grown up in the Midwest, Pastor Bartels views the collaborative, pragmatic ministry they have at Holy Cross as an implementation of "barnyard theology." As the head farmer or shepherd, he insists "all animals have their purpose on the farm. They each have a different role, but they are all still a part of the farm. And you never know which animal you might need to meet a certain challenge or need. You've just got to have all of them ready to go," he explains.

GOALS AND DESIRED OUTCOMES

While the mission remains vibrant at Holy Cross Lutheran Church and School, significant challenges confront their unified ministry in North Miami. A large public school exists across the street. Area charter schools compete for the same students. The Holy Cross campus is too small to have athletic fields, though it does have an outdoor playground and basketball courts. Athletic teams must limit practice time to daylight hours. Crime is more prevalent in the area compared to the early 1990s. "When we see a helicopter in the air," says Mackey, "we immediately go on lockdown." After being robbed and burglarized a few times, cameras and a video security system were installed. Since then, there have been no further burglaries.

Even as the campus is protected and secured by a fence and a vigilant administration and staff, the church and school clearly provide a safe haven and beacon of hope in the midst of an underserved community. Both church and school doors are open so they can minister to those in need. Food pantries are available and accessible for the poor and hungry. In addition to providing a safe, loving, and nurturing growth environment, students receive two free meals a day (breakfast and lunch), which makes a tangible difference in a poor neighborhood and for deprived socioeconomic households. Due to a fruitful partnership with Lutheran Special Education Ministry (LSEM), students with disabilities are welcomed and accepted at Holy Cross, one of the few parochial schools that provides this service. And, of course, a Christ-centered mission, which feeds young people the Gospel and gives them hope and purpose, blesses all students who enroll.

While the demographics and neighborhood have changed, the goals of Holy Cross Lutheran School have not. Their identity statement—"Holy Cross is a family who proclaims Jesus Christ as Lord and Savior through love, worship, education and service to all people"—remains vibrant and visibly clear. "We are a hospital for sinners," one teacher shares, "not a place for saints." Another staff member portrays Holy Cross as a Statue of Liberty in south Florida—a beacon of hope for a community that needs to know Jesus has set them free from their sins and has created them for purpose-filled lives. Another faculty member puts it simply: "We want to connect students to Jesus Christ." Indeed, the number-one objective is for students to learn more about God's Word and what Jesus Christ has done for them. "We want to present the Gospel message every day," explains an administrator, "and then let the Holy Spirit do His work." No student leaves the school without knowing that he or she is loved by God and the Holy Cross community.

Of course, many families send their children to Holy Cross without knowing anything about Jesus Christ, the Bible, or the Lutheran tradition. Holy Cross's reputation for being a safe school is a preeminent draw for many parents. They also want an aspirational and inspirational learning experience for their children—a place that will prepare their son or daughter for high school and put them on a path toward a better standard of living. The mission statement explains that "Holy Cross encourages academic excellence and a firm foundation in Christian faith through teaching and nurturing in partnership with students, staff, parents and community." Thus, closing the achievement gap certainly remains another primary focus. "We have a failing public school system," says one administrator. "Many parents send their kids here just to get a fair shot at academic success." Administration and faculty set high standards and expectations for their students, and Holy Cross retains an outstanding reputation for high school preparation as well as leadership skills and dispositional development. School officials are mindful that the expectations must be realistic based on the family dynamics of their community. In general, teachers assign about ten minutes of homework per grade level (e.g., a fifth-grade student might have fifty minutes of homework per night).

As students learn and practice the soft skills, leadership skills, and dispositions they need to be successful in everyday life, Holy Cross faculty members model a spirit of generosity to their students. "Teaching them to give is really hard," explains one teacher, "because of how truly needy most of them are." The number of alumni who come back to serve or volunteer in the school is one way faculty members measure and validate how well their teaching or lessons on generosity have stuck in the hearts and minds of their students.

Holy Cross teachers want their students to make an impact in their communities and create positive change. Therefore, modeling and teaching students grit, perseverance, resilience, how to deal with setbacks, and the value of hard work remain key focal points and constant threads of emphasis throughout the formal and hidden curriculum in the school.

While parents may send their children to Holy Cross Lutheran School for the safe and caring environment, leadership development, or academic readiness and preparation, the most critical objective for school leaders and teachers is to connect their students to Christ. Many students come from broken homes, abject poverty, neighborhoods infested with crime and drugs, families who want a better life for their children, or households where they receive insufficient love and attention. These students need to know Jesus' unconditional love for them. "To the weak I became weak, that I might win the weak," says the apostle Paul. "I have become all things to all people, that by all means I might save some. I do it all for the sake of the gospel, that I may share with them in its blessings" (1 Corinthians 9:22–23).

Inspired by God's Word, the administration, faculty, and staff of Holy Cross have fully adopted the notion that a flower can only bloom where it is planted.

> What then is Apollos? What is Paul? Servants through whom you believed, as the Lord assigned to each. I planted, Apollos watered, but God gave the growth. So neither he who plants nor he who waters is anything, but only God who gives the growth. He who plants and he who waters are one, and each will receive his wages according to his labor. For we are God's fellow workers. You are God's field, God's building. (1 Corinthians 3:5–9)

The mission field, God's field, for Holy Cross Lutheran Church and School is in North Miami. Great ministry is taking place each and every day in their school building. The mission field has indeed come to them. Too many other

Christian schools have closed around the urban fringe of Miami. "God gives you a mission field and you gotta recognize it," insists Pastor Bartels. By God's grace, the leaders and teachers of Holy Cross have been called to bloom where God has planted them, and they are boldly going forward in faith.

IMPLEMENTATION, RESULTS, AND ANALYSIS OF THE MISSION AND MINISTRY

While the key pillars of Holy Cross Lutheran School—safety, caring environment, academic preparedness, leadership and soft skills development, and the teaching of Christ and His Word—have not changed over the last two decades, the demographic shift has compelled school officials to modify and tweak their methods and tactics. No one master plan dominates their approach to school ministry. No one pivotal moment caused the school to dramatically shift or transform their approach to Lutheran education. Instead, Holy Cross leaders and staff members continue to make incremental, gradual, continuous, nonideological, and practical tweaks and adjustments over time. They craft changes after examining the needs in their community, reflecting upon their own successes and failures—their own action research—as new families and students settle in their community. This collaborative, staff-led ministry approach to the shared goals and desired ministry outcomes fosters a collective mind-set and, at the same time, encourages every individual to make modifications and changes, at any time, for the good of the students.

In the academic arena, for example, the goal of having kids prepared for high school success has never changed at Holy Cross. As more Haitians came to their school and the faculty learned that Creole was not an official written language until the twentieth century and does not have a cultural history emphasizing the importance of writing, the faculty and staff adjusted their approach and scheduled more time to teach writing and give their Haitian students more opportunities to write.

In terms of developing soft skills and leadership skills, the faculty and staff implemented specially designed field trips and excursions to expose their students to different cultural hotspots in the United States and American experience. Fourth and fifth graders now go on camping trips to learn about teamwork, communication, and serving others. Middle schoolers take an annual trip—which rotates from Florida (including stops at the Kennedy Space Center and Sea World) to the northeast (Boston, New York, Williamsburg, and Washington, DC) to Pennsylvania and Canada (Niagara Falls, Hershey, Amish country, Philadelphia)—where they experience different parts of the American landscape as well as practice and develop their listening, observation, communication, research, and service-learning skills. Middle school students also receive a cultural immersion experience that varies from year to year. Two decades ago, many area families could or would take their children on vacations and excursions outside of south Florida, even if just to visit family. The vast majority of Holy Cross's students today, however, would never leave south Florida if not for Holy Cross designing and executing these specific learning adventures.

In addition to these intentional excursions and trips, teachers are encouraged to take students off campus and into the community, where they can practice their learning in the real world. "One of the big things we emphasize," says one middle school teacher, "is that we expect our students to be well-behaved because the world is expecting something else of them." She particularly enjoys taking her students into the community quite frequently so that they can engage and interact with people of all different backgrounds, ages, and occupations. "Our principal is great about that," she explains. "There might be a great new documentary or play downtown that I would love for my kids to see. Even the trip downtown and riding on a bus all by itself is a great experience for my students. Sherri, our principal, trusts me and encourages me to give my students experiences that matter and prepare them for the real world. We all have that kind of academic freedom here at Holy Cross."

Students volunteer their time singing at area nursing homes, doing sign language at various civic events, and working with the local police department on neighborhood improvement projects and programs. Indeed, Holy Cross students experience and practice their interpersonal, leadership, and communication skills in a variety of real-world situations, which are recognized and appreciated by the community. Area high schools aggressively recruit Holy Cross students and families because of their interpersonal and leadership skills.

Holy Cross has not changed their commitment to their students' faith walk and growth. To enroll at the school, parents still must read a statement of faith and understand that their child will be receiving a Christian, Bible-based education with no apologies. Holy Cross takes the call in Matthew 19:14 seriously, where Jesus says, "Let the little children come to Me and do not hinder them, for to such belongs the kingdom of heaven." According to the Holy Cross statement of faith, students will receive "daily teachings from God's Holy Word" because "Holy Cross Lutheran School exists to help ground our students in the living Christian faith as taught by our Lord and Savior, Jesus Christ." Parents also must adhere to the Christian code of conduct. Students must "dress in conformance with one's biological sex, use the restrooms, locker rooms, and changing facilities conforming with one's biological sex, abstain from sexual conduct outside the marital union of one man and one woman," and cannot participate in "negative actions such as cheating, stealing, aggressive behavior, disruptive behavior, or lack of respect for authority."

While chapel has always been a staple of Holy Cross's ministry, they have administered some changes in this arena due to the new makeup of the student population. Once a month, the entire school, from preK to eighth grade, attends a mass chapel. During these chapels, students read the Apostles' Creed and an article of Luther's Small Catechism, all posted on large screens in front of the church sanctuary under the direction of Pastor Bartels. Bible verses are read aloud and a homily is given by Pastor Bartels or a trained LCMS church worker. A praise band leads the group in a few songs that are sung and celebrated with great energy and emotion. In addition to the mass monthly chapel, students attend weekly, customized chapel services for their age group, one for preK through second grade and one for third through eighth grade. Many Haitian students attend Baptist, Catholic, Pentecostal, and nondenominational churches with loud, lively, and upbeat contemporary worship formats, so a Lutheran chapel service is a new experience for them. Pastor Bartels has been very intentional in tweaking chapel to better engage students. Some families of these students come to Sunday morning worship services, though getting more to come to Sunday worship remains a challenge. Some students and families have different backgrounds and inaccurately believe they are not allowed to worship at Holy Cross Lutheran Church because they are not members. Different social customs and misunderstandings like this one remain a social barrier that Holy Cross Lutheran Church and School work to overcome.

While many of the veteran administrators and faculty members have seen remarkable change in their community, they remain adamant about the non-negotiables of doing ministry in the urban fringe. These nonnegotiables, or core values, are conspicuous everywhere on campus. First, to meet the dire and pressing needs of their families, the faculty and staff of Holy Cross are determined to live and do ministry together as a family. Everyone, after all, is a child of God, and God is the holy Father of all. Every child, no matter their background or ethnicity, is welcomed with loving and open arms. Second, unconditional love remains at the forefront of almost everything they do. They teach students how to make God-pleasing decisions. More important, they model *agape* love—a committed and sacrificial love, inspired by Christ, that students can eventually embrace in their own family or wherever they may go. Third, the faculty and staff do all they can to support students after they graduate from Holy Cross. They invite graduates to volunteer and give back to the school. They stay connected to alumni through social media, always looking for opportunities to bring them back so that they share their high school, college, or life experiences with Holy Cross students. Finally, teachers remain passionate and committed to their student's academic growth and connecting their kids to Christ and His Holy Word.

LESSONS FROM HOLY CROSS

Holy Cross Lutheran School faces many challenges. While well-maintained, nostalgic, and beautiful—especially the two outdoor campus courtyards—the original 1951 facility is aging and showing wear. Moreover, the school is landlocked and does not have athletic fields for practice or to host sporting events. The gym/cafeteria is cramped, not suitable for most athletic competitions, and does not have the modern amenities that so many other taxpayer-funded schools take for granted. Sports teams practice on the outdoor concrete courts but must complete their workouts before sundown. "Students have to practice outside right after school and then study when they are tired," notes Beverly Thompson, the athletic director. "We wish it could be the other way around." She adds with a wink: "We all play the lotto once a week around here, because we need to hit it big and expand this campus." As enrollment increases, the lack of space becomes more challenging. Offices are small or nonexistent, classrooms are tight, and storage is in great demand. Since demographic turnover and change have been the norm in North Miami, some staff members worry that the Step Up for Students scholarship funding, which provides tuition funding for over 75 percent of Holy Cross families, could go away due to misinformation in the public sector and political pressures. Federal and state government regulations and bureaucracy continue to create unnecessary frustrations. One family seeking Title I funding, for example, put "North Miami" instead of "Miami" on their application. They could not receive funds for this innocent mistake even when the family rectified the error. The faculty and staff wish more resources were available to invest further in STEM education and teacher aides in order to increase the academic standards. Finding extra funding to hire a social worker or two would also help families navigate social services—assistance many need desperately. Perhaps the greatest challenge, however, is raising or recruiting future administrators and teachers. When they have hired promising candidates and invested in their growth and development in the past, many left after short durations for other ministry or career opportunities. Finding LCMS-trained church workers, or even other Christ-centered individuals, who are interested in and prepared for ministry in an urban setting, let alone in south Florida, remains a daunting challenge and significant concern.

Though many challenges exist, Holy Cross Lutheran School is a humble, shining oasis of love and hope for so many families and students living in the North Miami area. Here are some lessons other Christian schools and leaders can learn from Holy Cross:

◆ *Remind yourself again that Jesus is your primary motivator in ministry.* As Pastor Bartels tells the faculty and staff of Holy Cross, their ministry is like a container full of mixed nuts—nuts that come in all different sizes, colors, and shapes, some healthier than others. They are all nuts nonetheless. In the same way, the faculty, staff, and students of Holy Cross are all different individuals with unique backgrounds, personal biographies, gifts, and challenges. Perhaps you are more comfortable "doing ministry" with people who look, sound, talk, and act like you. Remember, however, that Jesus came to die for all people. All people are God's children made in His image. Thus, remind yourself to heed God's Word: "Go therefore and make disciples of all nations, baptizing them in the name of the Father and of the Son and of the Holy Spirit, teaching them to observe all that I have commanded you. And behold, I am with you always, to the end of the age" (Matthew 28:18–20).

◆ *Make sure pastor and principal invest in building a strong relationship with each other.* Ministry and life are tough enough, especially when dealing with challenging socioeconomic issues and enduring the devil's attacks. If you are an administrator, seek your pastor's support and share your vulnerabilities with him. If you are a pastor, take time to encourage and build up your administrator. Come together in prayer and Bible study. Respect and affirm each other's gifts and vocations. A unified mission between church and school can only occur when it is centered on Christ. There are few things more inspiring in a school ministry than when a pastor lifts up and supports his administrator and vice versa. In a ministry dependent on deep, trustworthy relationships at all levels, the pastor must trust his administrator to do whatever it takes to employ effective school ministry practices. At the same time, the administrator should seek spiritual counsel and support from his or her pastor to ensure a harmonious missional focus.

◆ *Expect and demand the best from the students God has put in your care.* Do not set lower standards or expectations for students simply because of their background, ethnicity, or socioeconomic status. Set high achievement standards and demand that your students learn and develop important lifelong skills. Embrace a growth mind-set, not a fixed one. (For more on a growth mind-set, see Carol Dweck's work.) Perhaps students are not up to grade level competencies or don't know the difference between Law and Gospel—not yet anyway. Both in academic matters and theological comprehension, welcome the growth mind-set that underserved students can develop their reading or math skills and learn the teachings of the Bible and Jesus Christ. Academic learning and religious understanding, however, will only improve and grow through hard work, a determined faculty and staff, and receiving God's Word and His grace. Many educators and parents say they want the best for their students. If you truly want the best for your students, then make sure you teach them God's Word and grace before all the rest. Do not settle for giving them anything less than the best and greatest of all time—their Savior, Jesus Christ.

◆ *Model and teach the behaviors and dispositions essential for future success and faithfulness.* Since many underserved students come from dysfunctional homes, they do not see critical traits and habits modeled or implemented on daily basis, but these are crucial for life success and a fruitful spiritual life. In particular, make sure your faculty and staff model a spirit of generosity, grit, resilience, persistence, relentless work ethic, forgiveness, faithful church attendance, Bible study, and Christ's love and compassion. You may not have a lot of money to invest in new programs, new technology, or new facilities, but you do have, thanks to Jesus, an unlimited amount of love and elbow grease to give.

◆ *Demonstrate, reveal, and show students success stories as well as inspiring faith stories.* Underserved students need to hear and see real success and real faith stories. Bring in guest speakers, alumni, and people in the community who have experienced success in the secular world and are also faithful, servant-minded Christians. Remember, too, that just being a Christ-centered professional at school—whether it be a teacher, custodian, secretary, administrator, or buildings and grounds employee—is a powerful example of success and faithfulness to young kids. Show and teach your students the difference between earthly success and God-fearing faithfulness. Both are desirable, but only one is essential for eternal salvation.

◆ *Hire or call individuals who understand and represent the makeup, mind-set, and ideology of your area families and students and who want to be fully invested in your culture and community.* Finding Christian administrators and teachers who have the right disposition, leadership, and pedagogical skills to serve in an urban setting is no easy task. Invest your time up front to build a network of potential teacher and administrator candidates and pipelines that meet your personnel and contextual needs.

◆ *Pursue friendships outside of your usual "group" or "tribe" to learn more about another culture.* If you do not know much about

Haitian people or Haitian culture, for example, be intentional about building a friendship with a Haitian colleague, parent, or congregation member with whom you can ask questions and learn without hesitation, embarrassment, or inhibition. Listen, learn, and let God work on your heart to develop a greater capacity for empathy and understanding.

◆ *Know which traditions to cling to and which ones to discard.* The adage "innovate or die" is not just for industries. Churches and Christian schools should heed this warning too—not in regard to doctrine or biblical teachings, but in how they connect and engage with a rapidly changing society and a postmodern culture inundated with pagan values. Hold fast to the truths of Scripture and never compromise the Gospel message. On the other hand, reevaluate your outreach and pedagogical methods so that you can adapt to the mission field of your neighborhood. What may work one year may not work the next. Be nimble and flexible to meet the shifting demographics of your community so that you are suitably prepared to welcome new students and parents to your Christian family.

◆ *Bloom where God plants you.* God has placed you and your ministry where you are for a reason. Perhaps you have to reinvent your delivery system or the ways you connect with your community. Whatever the context or situation, be open to change and embrace it. Every child is a child of God, and everyone has an opportunity to share the love of Jesus. The Holy Spirit knows no bounds, and God's Word will never return to Him empty but will accomplish His purposes and plans (Isaiah 55:11). Remember how exciting and special it is that God allows children to enter your school ministry and learn about the love and blessings of Christ. You get to be His tool and instrument and watch your students grow and bloom in God's grace and love. What a joy-filled ministry and vocation God has given you!

Holy Cross Lutheran School may be located on the fringe of urban Miami, but they remain at the center of a missionary outpost God has established for them. Like Esther so many centuries ago, they have been planted to serve and bloom right where they are "for such a time as this" (Esther 4:14).

3   "Yes, We Can"

THE COLLEGE PREPARATORY MODEL:

CREAN LUTHERAN HIGH SCHOOL
IRVINE, CA

The Challenge and Opportunity: Designing a College Preparatory School in the Twenty-First Century

Driving onto the campus of Crean Lutheran High School (CLHS), one notices the canopy of trees that shade the entrance road in a Savannah, Georgia, look. The cool covering in sunny California certainly portends something unique. Continuing on "the road to Damascus," as some faculty members refer to it, one cannot help but see the huge, rugged cross planted in the ground at the turn, green trees and shrubs providing a spectacular contrast and background that only accentuates Christianity's most important symbol. The splendid landscape and cross remind passengers of the sacrifice made by their beautiful Savior, Jesus Christ.

With over eight hundred students, the "miracle" of CLHS is now entering its second decade. Rapid enrollment spurred brisk development on the thirty-acre campus. The buildings and athletic fields look and feel contemporary even as numerous building projects and campus enhancements continue unabated. On the north end of the main campus, a new school village appears, consisting of separate drama, choir, band, and dance studios, along with a new arts and athletics building, academic building, strength and conditioning center, and a training field. Soon a new gymnasium will emerge on the campus too. As enrollment is expected and projected to grow, CLHS continues to move forward in faith, confident in their mission and God's provision.

Residing in the well-to-do city of Irvine and the hypercompetitive academic setting of Orange County, California—on average, eight to ten students in area high schools score perfect ACT scores annually—CLHS executive director Jeffrey Beavers often finds himself trying to meet the needs and requests of potential students and their families. During the last decade, for example, CLHS has earned a reputation for being the high school of choice for world-class swimmers—many receiving division one scholarships and five having participated in Olympic trials. The families of these talented swimmers were not initially drawn to the school's athletic program (their competitive swimming interests are off-site). Instead, they enrolled their children because of the excellent academic reputation and the school's willingness to accommodate their child's scheduling needs. Internationally competitive swimmers must practice and compete all over the United States without being inhibited by traditional school schedules. In other words, these student-athletes cannot be in school every day from September to June. They will miss chunks of time—sometimes weeks—while they practice and compete sometimes thousands of miles away. The traditional school calendar will not work for them. They need a personalized schedule. So when the parents of these swimmers asked for a customized schedule, CLHS administrators listened to the request, looked these parents in the eyes, and responded, "Yes, we can."

"We say yes a lot," says Beavers. "We try to listen and act on the needs of people without compromising the main tenets and core of our ministry and rigor." This attitude, or formula, has served CLHS well for over a decade and remains an intentional disposition of the school. "Back when we started out with eighty-five students in our first year," recalls Beavers, the founding principal of the school, "we never made the excuse that we couldn't start a program or begin a tradition because we were too small. We never said, 'We should wait until enrollment grows.' From dances to performing arts to athletics to yearbook to student life, we always valued the students we had and did everything we could to make their high school experience excellent. We still do."

THE CREAN LUTHERAN STORY

The launch of a Lutheran high school has always been a formidable undertaking, but perhaps more so in the twenty-first century, when the costs of employee benefits, land, and building materials often increase faster than inflation in many parts of the country. Moreover, there are more educational options for parents and high schoolers to choose from today than ever before.

But John and Donna Crean, along with several other faithful supporters, had a dream to start a new Lutheran high school. In 2007, a few years after creating all the necessary infrastructure and housing students in a local Greek orthodox church, the John and Donna Crean Foundation committed the transformational gift of ten million dollars for a new Lutheran high school facility. Named after these benefactors, Crean Lutheran High School also embraces the "CREAN (**C**hrist **R**edeems **E**ducates **A**nd **N**urtures!) Way." In the fall of 2007, CLHS welcomed nearly one hundred students to campus. Because the school has over eight hundred students today, one might think that the increase in student enrollment seemed inevitable and predictable when the school started over a decade ago. For the founders, faculty, and staff of CLHS, however, the fact that approximately one hundred students were added each of the first seven years after the school opened remains an essential part of the "miracle" story of CLHS. Indeed, the Great Recession of 2008–2010, the worst economic downturn in US history since the Great Depression, hit southern California particularly hard. In the midst of the brutal economic environment and tough academic competition in Orange County, local supporters and church workers insist that CLHS is an incredible story of God's faithfulness. They credit Him for removing the barriers to the school's launch and growth. Favorable loans from the Lutheran Church Extension Fund (LCEF) and Thrivent Financial for Lutherans further nurtured and supported the growth of CLHS. Soon after opening their new facility, more acres of land were purchased for athletic fields and campus expansion. Today, the campus consists of thirty acres as the school continues to construct building additions to meet all of the various needs of their programming and student body.

In 2012, the National Lutheran School Association (NLSA) recognized CLHS as one of its "exemplary schools." Success in athletics and arts soon followed. The school also launched its highly anticipated academic cohort programs in the fall of 2013—initially a medical cohort with engineering and business cohorts soon added. In 2015, CLHS became the third largest Lutheran high school in the country. In 2016, the *Washington Post* recognized the institution as one of the "Most Challenging Private Schools in America" based on their students' Advanced Placement (AP) results from the prior year. The average ACT score of CLHS students is well above the state and national averages at 25 or higher. Several students each year are commended for the National

Merit Program. As graduates continue to receive lucrative scholarships and gain admittance into top public and private universities from coast to coast, CLHS also continues to earn accolades for being one of the best one-stop-shop college preparatory schools in the country.

GOALS AND DESIRED OUTCOMES OF A COLLEGE PREPARATORY PROGRAM

Skeptics question if a parochial school can focus on two formidable goals—rigorously preparing students for elite college success *and* teaching the Christian faith throughout one's academic and cocurricular programming. Indeed, the danger and temptation of serving humankind or worldly desires is that it can distract and prohibit one from also serving the Lord (Galatians 1:10).

Alas, the temptation of mission drift is something that CLHS leadership, faculty, and staff talk about frequently in their daily morning Bible studies as well as in their strategic planning sessions. The key, as they see it, is keeping their eye intensely focused on their mission, which is "Proclaiming Jesus Christ through Excellence in Education." Proclaiming Christ must always be the prime objective, and they can do this through the platform built on a reputation of academic excellence. CLHS officials constantly dialogue about how their labor would be in vain and meaningless if the programs, buildings, and academic successes would supersede the mission.

The mission and vision of CLHS are bold and clear to be sure. The school does not shy away from its commitment to be both an excellent college-preparatory school *and* a Christ-centered one at the same time. The vision statements of CLHS insist that their school must be "a beacon which shines the light of Jesus Christ in a world of spiritual darkness" and a "transformational experience for its students as they matriculate into disciples of Jesus Christ." Their teachers, as inspired by the Holy Spirit, will establish "an exceptional educational framework that is innovative, future-oriented and responsive to the changing demands and needs of high school students in an increasingly complex and technologically advancing world" and pursue "best educational practices." CLHS desires to have each student learn and celebrate "God's redemptive love and grace" and "pass on the Gospel" to others. They will "become productive, responsible citizens whose growing relationship with

Jesus Christ enables them to fulfill God's purpose in their daily lives and in their ultimate vocations."

Visible everywhere around campus, in hallways and classrooms, is the acronym CLS, which stands for "Christian, Learner, Servant." By the time they graduate, students are expected to have a close relationship with Jesus Christ, embrace lifelong learning, and serve others because Christ first served them. Many Lutheran schools claim the same themes. But from the largest to the smallest detail, the intentionality of CLHS team members is visible as they daily live the school's mission. Indeed, many faculty and staff members are quick to note Colossians 3:23–24: "Whatever you do, work heartily, as for the Lord and not for men, knowing that from the Lord you will receive the inheritance as your reward. You are serving the Lord Christ."

IMPLEMENTATION, RESULTS, AND ANALYSIS OF THE ONE-STOP-SHOP COLLEGE PREPARATORY APPROACH

The lifeblood of any Lutheran school is hiring and retaining Christ-centered teachers. With the shortage of trained Lutheran Church—Missouri Synod (LCMS) teachers, only 25 percent of the CLHS staff is made up of rostered LCMS workers. Thus, CLHS has designed a thorough hiring process, where each teacher candidate goes through three sets of interviews—one with members of the department, one with the administrative team, and finally one with the executive director. Before the final interview with the executive director, teacher candidates are taken out to lunch with current teachers, who size up the individual's social skills, emotional intelligence, and mission fit. The interview teams pay particularly close attention to the prospective teacher's transparency and authenticity about his or her faith.

Once hired, the expectation is that teachers will grow in their Christian faith, content knowledge, and instructional capabilities. Regarding the shortage of high-quality Christian teachers, Beavers says, "Everyone is searching for all-stars, but we believe in building our own all-stars." On the instructional and academic side of things, CLHS provides teachers with adequate resources and then tries to place them in their sweet spots so that they can grow and become subject matter experts. CLHS also encourages and expects teachers to be dedicated to their relationship with Jesus Christ. If the school expects students to grow in their faith through intentional Bible study and prayer, so too must teachers. Put another way, if teachers are growing in their faith, then their students are likely to follow.

One of the first things the faculty and staff do at the start of each school year is read the mission statement ("Proclaiming Jesus Christ through Excellence in Education") and motto of the school (Decidedly Christian! Distinctively Excellent!) and engage in reflective discussions on how best to bring both to fruition in the coming school year. Each team member is encouraged to attend devotions every morning, and faculty and staff are also asked to lead at least two of these devotions for the group. The intent is to provide many opportunities for faculty and staff to grow in their own spiritual journey and to get comfortable leading others in their faith walk too. Everyone—staff, faculty, and administrators—are asked for input in the vision and vision implementation of the school. "I like to think of keeping teachers in touch with and highly involved with stretching the vision, like someone might stretch a rubber band without breaking it," says Beavers. This form of distributed leadership builds ownership in the mission and vision.

No matter how focused the administration, faculty, and staff remain on the Christ-centered mission, however, the reality in the twenty-first century is that many prospective families do not consider the faith-based focus of a school to be a main drawing card. This is where the mission statement—"Proclaiming Jesus Christ *through Excellence in Education*" (italics added)—serves as a mission opportunity for CLHS. While only 40 percent of the students are Lutheran, 98 percent of CLHS graduates go on to a two- or four-year college. Most overcrowded public schools in Orange County have student-teacher ratios as high as 45:1. In addition, more students from the Pacific Rim and Middle Eastern countries continue to enroll. Standing out as a leading college preparatory school has allowed the mission field to come to the CLHS campus, hallways, and classrooms despite tuition and fees that could purchase a compact automobile in the Midwest. The academic programming and desire to fulfill the needs and hopes of area families and students in the temporal (e.g., helping students receive a significant scholarship or admittance into an elite college) can be used as platform to share and teach something of significance for the eternal—God's Word and redemption through Jesus Christ. In this manner,

CLHS can serve families both for this life and the next. Put another way, having a distinctively excellent academic program attracts students who eventually graduate knowing that their Redeemer lives.

In addition to having talented, growth-minded, dedicated church workers, a Lutheran college preparatory high school must pursue academic excellence intentionally and daily. For CLHS, it's not just what they attempt to do but how and why they do it. Here are some important aspects of the overall academic approach of CLHS:

- The student's academic journey starts with a dynamic college and career planning experience and an individualized plan tailored to each student's interests and strengths. CLHS has five full-time, credentialed counselors who meet with each student frequently throughout his or her four years. These Christ-centered counselors guide students toward God's plan for them (Jeremiah 29:11), help them discover their gifts and talents, and encourage them to live a life of purpose in Jesus' name.

- A weekly email, the "Counseling Corner," is sent out to inform parents of upcoming college recruiter visits and scholarship opportunities. The email also educates parents and provides important tips on the college search and admission process.

- All freshmen are required to take a Cornerstone class, usually in the summer before their freshman year, to get a head start on planning their academic future. The Cornerstone curriculum includes personality research and discovery, strengths testing (StrengthsQuest by Gallup), résumé building, college fairs, college search tips and information, and learning what it means to be a digital citizen, how to create a digital footprint, and other student success training—such as time management, study skills, organization, time blocking, stress management, conflict resolution, learning and applying a Christian worldview, and servant leadership. Students study and absorb the intricacies of the school's mission and vision statements, chapel, and desired learning outcomes. In addition, the class provides a special orientation of CLHS so students can hit the ground running on the first day of their freshman year.

◆ All students are offered the opportunity to take Princeton Review SAT and ACT preparation courses, which include fifteen hours of specialized test training. The $1,200 cost of this course is included in each student's tuition.

◆ Throughout their tenure at CLHS, many students take four scheduled trips to different universities to learn the language of higher education and what to look for in the college application and admission processes.

◆ Numerous workshops are offered and organized so students can improve and enhance their writing and interview skills.

◆ A college application boot camp is provided for all students the summer preceding their senior year. A comprehensive review of the entire application process is covered in great detail. Students know what they must prepare for, do, and complete in the admission process. They also gain awareness and confidence in pursuing their career vocations, scholarships, and universities of choice.

◆ A comprehensive website, Naviance Family Connection, provides students and families access to track and analyze data about college and career planning. Naviance presents up-to-date information specific to CLHS. In addition, this tool assists families and students in building a résumé, managing timelines and deadlines for making decisions about colleges and careers, comparing information between colleges, assessing the current job market and potential job markets of future careers, and creating goals and to-do lists in order to make educational dreams come to fruition. Furthermore, Naviance shares information about upcoming meetings and events, local scholarship opportunities, and college and career information.

◆ Once a month, while CLHS faculty and staff engage in a professional development day, students stay at home and participate in a mandatory online learning day. They believe all students should experience learning in a blended, online delivery format.

◆ Approximately 10 percent of CLHS students participate in hybrid classes, attending school on either Mondays, Wednesdays, and

Fridays or on Tuesdays, Thursdays, and Fridays. Since CLHS has Blue and Gold days (a block schedule of longer, college-like periods), students in this program, for example, might take four classes on campus on Blue days, while working on their online courses at home through CLHS or another accredited institution on Gold days. This format is not only a cheaper option for some families (online courses at other accredited institutions generally cost less than a face-to-face class at CLHS), but it also provides schedule flexibility to parents and students engaged in other activities that require odd practice times or out-of-town training experiences and competitions (e.g., swimming, fencing, snowboarding, and tae kwon do).

◆ The curriculum includes 21 Advanced Placement (AP) courses, 32 honors courses, and 25 dual-credit courses. Students who are not taking multiple AP, honors, or dual-credit courses are the exception to the academic rule at CLHS.

◆ Students are able to join three prestigious cohort programs in the medical, engineering, and business fields. Future cohorts in law and human development are currently being considered. These value-added cohorts are designed for highly motivated students who seek to learn more about these specific fields from professionals and immersion experiences. They also discover whether they want to pursue the field further in college. Cohort students conduct independent research, attend lectures given by professionals in the industry, participate in hands-on learning labs from a Christian perspective, take field trips to dynamic and innovative workplace settings (e.g., IBM, Disneyland), and complete a minimum of 125 hours in an internship. Students who complete all four years in one cohort receive special graduation cords as well as a special distinction on their transcripts.

◆ The Ambassador Internship program embeds students in numerous professional development seminars and provides hands-on experiences as they work with the school's External Relations department in areas of advancement, recruitment, congregational and community relationships, and public relations.

◆ The Learning Success program delivers customized learning strategies and skill development sessions designed to foster independence and personal academic growth in students. The program offers specific learning accommodations and hands-on assistance across all content areas.

◆ In addition to Life Groups, where teachers lead groups of students on faith projects in the community, and annual mission trips to locations such as Mexico, Cuba, El Salvador, and Hungary, students are also encouraged to practice and develop their leadership skills as part of the Servant Leadership Team.

◆ Students can also participate in over fifty active student clubs or create their own at CLHS.

A CASE STUDY WITHIN A CASE STUDY: THE INTERNATIONAL STUDENT PROGRAM OF CLHS

CLHS's commitment to their mission and the creation of a one-stop shop is clearly evident in their international student program. Just as Jesus sent fish into the disciples' net on the Sea of Galilee (John 21:1–6), God continues to bring the mission field to CLHS. Over 20 percent of the student body of CLHS is made up of students from twenty different countries, primarily South Korea and China. The fact that Irvine, California, is a sunny, beautiful city enriched by a wealthy, diverse community certainly attracts many international families and students. Moreover, CLHS invests in reaching out to these well-to-do international students and families, certainly to increase their enrollment and revenue stream, but also to share the Gospel with these children of God. Sadly, many Chinese families have never read the Bible. A Christian education initially has little allure to international families who are simply seeking the best of Western education. CLHS found out very early in its inception, however, that if you promote your school's academic success and highlight the rigorous SAT/ACT test preparation included in the curriculum, then you win an audience or platform where you can share and teach about Jesus to international students too.

International students attending CLHS must meet or surpass TOEFL (Test of English as a Foreign Language) proficiency standards. CLHS provides TOEFL classes on Fridays, as well as an intensive introductory and immersion program for four consecutive weeks over the summer, so that international students can improve their reading and writing skills and come to better understand CLHS, its mission, and its offerings. If an international student earns a B grade or lower, his or her parents receive a personal phone call from the international student director.

In the future, CLHS will slightly lower the percentage of international students to ensure quality control and better efficiencies within its academic infrastructure and program. The school only enrolls I-20 international students who are committed to a four-year duration. CLHS does not put international students in ESL (English as a Second Language) classes because many find the reference demeaning. Instead, CLHS enrolls I-20 students in writing and communication courses.

Like many Lutheran high schools, the theology curriculum and course sequence at CLHS follows an Old Testament, New Testament, Christian Doctrine, and World Religions/Apologetics track for freshman, sophomore, junior, and senior year respectively. International students, however, are first assessed as to their knowledge of Christ and may instead take a special Introduction to Christianity course, which deploys a Sunday School approach to teaching—using more visuals and covering the more well-known biblical accounts and stories. Faculty members found the Old Testament course too rigorous and intimidating for many international students who have limited prior knowledge of the Bible. Spending three hours a night to study the Old Testament frustrated many international students and turned them off of Bible study in general. The introductory course—led by a caring, approachable, mission-minded instructor—made sense not only academically but also as an evangelical mission fit.

While many international students first come to CLHS unchurched and agnostic, they leave or graduate knowing God's Word and the saving grace of Jesus Christ. This is no small victory considering the cultural context and pagan pressures many Asians feel living away from their native cultures and home. "Please don't tell my parents I go to church," more than one Chinese student has told CLHS officials when their parents come from overseas to visit. Due to decades of the horrific one-child policy in China, many of CLHS's Chinese students graduate from a US high school or college but return home to run the family business. They are often the only family member qualified to do so. More important, when they return to China, these CLHS alumni feel emboldened and compelled to share the Gospel. Some have even opened their own Christian schools.

In a world that lacks people loving people, CLHS's dual focus of preparing students for success in college *and* an eternal life with Christ seems to have found the mark for students and families in Orange County and across the globe.

LESSONS FROM A ONE-STOP ACADEMIC SHOP

Before sharing lessons other Christian schools and Christian leaders can glean from Crean, let us examine the "yeah buts" first. *Yeah*, CLHS is an accomplished school, *but* ours would be too if we lived in a wealthy zip code and growing area where we could charge a higher tuition. *Yeah*, all the extra college counseling and career planning is impressive, *but* we do not have CLHS's resources or enrollment to do the college preparatory one-stop-shop approach. *Yeah*, some of their academic programming and cohort models are intriguing, *but* we do not have the same talented community network to draw from or the administrative bandwidth. *Yeah*, they're big, *but* we're small. *Yeah*, they are wealthy, *but* we are financially strapped.

There may be truth to all of these "yeah buts" and comparisons. All schools have challenges and can make excuses for not acting. CLHS's intentionality and efforts to say yes to the academic and collegiate desires of potential families obliged school leadership to borrow money and acquire loans while investing in land, personnel, and educational resources (classrooms, athletic fields, fine arts facilities, etc.). To service their debt, CLHS officials certainly feel the pressure to annually increase enrollment. Moreover, the innate challenges that come from growth—keeping up with infrastructure in personnel and facilities and always being mindful of mission drift—are real and formidable. The leadership of CLHS, however, remains vigilant. They realize Satan has a strategic plan for their school too. Lead administrators, as well as faculty and staff, constantly converse in faculty "family" meetings about the temptations of Satan and not losing sight of their collective calling and Christian mission.

No matter your school size or setting, there is much to embrace and learn from the Crean Way:

- *Find ways to say yes to the needs of your community and families.* Perhaps you or your school do not feel ready to say yes to every community desire or every family's wish list. You can, however, start developing the discipline and strategic mind-set to say yes more often than no. Saying no is quick and easy and often gives leaders a false sense of prioritization. But saying no also sends the message that you do not care enough to meet the needs and interests of your community or families, especially those who may not have any affiliation or connection to Christians and Christianity. Is this the message you want to send—that Christians or Christian schools frankly do not give a darn about families' needs and wants? Instead, say yes and put your trust and faith in God. As Jesus said, "With God all things are possible" (Matthew 19:26). Show your enthusiasm to serve by listening to people's wants and needs and then doing the best you can to meet them. Your yes may also lead to deeper thinking and innovative practices— something better than you ever expected. God is sending the mission field to your neighborhood. Are you excited and willing to minister to the parents and students Jesus sends your way?

- *Use academic excellence as a platform and beacon to share and teach God's Word and the Christian faith.* Excellence of any kind makes people notice. For Christians, Jesus is the inspiration to pursue excellence in all vocations. After all, Jesus gave His very best (perfect) blood on the cross so that our sins would be forgiven. Thus, be open and inspired to find your academic niche and platform. Show your community families that excellence is not limited to their child doing well in school but extends to being well in life—present and future. Worldly knowledge and skill development are necessary and highly desirable for college and twenty-first-century jobs, but God's wisdom and Word are more important and provide a peace that surpasses all human understanding and, eventually, eternal life. Show and persuade families of the benefit of an excellent, Christ-centered education.

◆ *Dedicate time to rereading your school's mission and vision statements—the why of your ministry and what mission accomplished looks like.* Even the best and most focused church workers should be challenged to grow spiritually and be reminded of the most important thing they teach and share. Your school is supposed to be radically and divinely different from the secular, government-run school down the street. In addition to rereading the mission and vision statements, unpack different parts of the statements and have small- and large-group discussions on what the mission means to each team member. Talk about ways each team member is planning to teach and live the mission in his or her class or co-curricular.

◆ *Make your mission and vision statements, student learner outcomes, and discipleship indicators visible and prominent in your school.* Many Lutheran schools publicize their mission statement or post a Bible verse on their school entrance or website, but everywhere you look on the CLHS website and campus—hallways, classroom and locker room walls, school transportation vans, coffee mugs, thank-you cards, recruitment brochures, even in the bathrooms— one quickly notices the mission statement, vision statements, CLS (Christian, Learner, Servant), or Bible verses prominently displayed. This is not only an intentional way to witness and share the faith but also a constant reminder to administration, faculty, and staff to stay focused and centered on teaching Jesus Christ and His Word. In a postmodern world where truth is considered subjective, the confidence and boldness of CLHS's message shines brightly and clearly. A seeking family just might think, Instead of falling for any societal trend, this school, at the very least, stands for something! Many people today still judge a book by its cover and schools by their walls. Since all school walls talk, what are yours saying?

◆ *Be on the lookout for mission drift and areas your school may be vulnerable for mission drift.* The administration and faculty of CLHS meet every morning for faculty devotions and Bible study. Staying in the Word keeps your team members centered and focused on Christ and a Christ-centered mission. Great leaders are willing to be vulnerable in front of their people. Be candid with one another in discussing ways your school may be tempted or distracted from doing God's work. Remind one another that busyness and living for one's own desires are two of Satan's most lethal weapons in detaching Christians and Christian institutions from God and His will.

◆ *Build depth and expertise in one area of your academic programming and expand from there.* Whether it be new cohort programming, upgraded academic counseling services, a Cornerstone class, blended learning curriculum, a commitment to dual-credit course offerings, or an enhanced international student endeavor, find one area to significantly upgrade in your academic programming. As you work to develop and enhance this initiative, other programs and faculty members will benefit from the spin-offs— the inspiration, the commitment to excellence, and the drive for continuous improvement. As Proverbs 27:17 asserts, "Iron sharpens iron, and one man sharpens another."

◆ *Keep your strategic plans nimble.* Good stewards are dedicated to strategic planning and executing the strategic plan. Some of Jesus' best ministry moments, however, came when He got interrupted. Be ready to embrace the spontaneous and unpredictable for ministry moments God sends your way. Say, "Yes, we can," to those special opportunities.

◆ *Survey your parents at least once a year and your students twice a year.* CLHS administrators, faculty, and staff constantly talk about and reflect on how they can improve. They are not satisfied with "good enough." To check off the boxes on student and parent checklists, you need to ask about the progress on the checklist or even if the checklist has changed. Getting honest, frequent feedback from parents and students has been a key in CLHS's rise and success.

◆ *Strive to be a one-stop shop, and "Jesus-proof" your school as you prepare the next generation of Christian leaders.* While CLHS desires to be a one-stop shop for college preparation and career planning, your context may be very different. The one-stop-shop approach, however, can and should be every Lutheran school's goal in regard to the sharing and teaching of the Christian faith. Being excellent in mission work never dumbs down educational work—quite the contrary in fact. Have your leadership bring in outsiders to conduct a faith audit to assess how well your school is truly teaching and integrating God's Word in all its truth and purity in every aspect of your curriculum and cocurriculars. Review your curriculum and make sure it adequately addresses the entire spectrum of a student's faith walk—from those who have never met Jesus or been exposed to God's Word to those who are ready to learn deep doctrine and rich apologetics as they contend for the faith. CLHS's administration, faculty, and staff make intentional efforts to "Jesus-proof" everything—that is, to ensure Jesus is the focus and reason for their work and improvements, like how a proof coin goes through a special process to make it more perfect. Whether creating a new brochure, classroom wall, presentation to parents, or daily lesson plans, CLHS officials encourage one another to remain vigilant and resolute in sharing Jesus and teaching God's Word in all that they do.

At the end of each day, CLHS students leave campus via the "Road to Damascus," past the huge rugged cross—implanted on school grounds but also, by the power of the Holy Spirit, in their hearts too. They are more prepared for college, life, and most important, the eternal life to come. That's the Crean Lutheran Way.

"A School That Nurtures Innovators and Groundbreakers"

4

THE STUDENT-CENTERED SCHOOL:

RENTON PREP AND AMAZING GRACE SCHOOLS
SEATTLE, WA

The Challenge and Opportunity: Declining Enrollment and a New Vision

In 1993, Amazing Grace Christian Elementary School set itself up for growth after previously downsizing to one prekindergarten class. The current pastor and his wife, a gifted educator in her own right, made the difficult decision to downsize the school amid many challenges. Then, they reembraced the challenge and opportunity of Lutheran education, rebuilding the school one grade at a time from kindergarten through fifth grade. From there, the school gradually blossomed into one of the most innovative models of Lutheran education in the nation, garnering visitors from around the United States and other parts of the world. They are drawing from the best and most current research on the science of teaching and learning, innovating and designing effective solutions, encouraging authentic projects, inviting students to learn through rich and authentic experiences, and building a mentor/mentee model that dominates much of what they do.

THE RENTON PREP SCHOOL STORY

Renton Prep Middle and High School is an extension of the Amazing Grace Christian Elementary School program. Out of all the stories told in this text, Renton Prep represents what is perhaps the most innovative when it comes to teaching and learning. Therefore, even though there are many aspects to the Renton Prep story, this chapter will devote the majority of attention to their innovative teaching and learning. It will also provide a few important insights about the context in which the school operates, a useful part of understanding what is truly distinct, even unique, about this Microsoft Showcase School, a rare distinction among public or private schools around the world. It is increasingly becoming a model for other schools as a place that is not afraid to try new things, a place where students love coming to school and where they are finding their voices.

As a school community, Renton Prep is distinct in many ways, but it starts with the leadership and teachers. As explained by the director of the school, teachers at Renton Prep love talking about education—building off of one another, challenging one another, collaborating with one another, and mentoring one another. There is a palpable camaraderie that is fueled by a shared mission and a common passion for the art and science of teaching and learning.

This teacher community is an important part of the Renton Prep distinction because what is modeled and experienced by teachers is quite similar to what they do with learners as well. The director explained that new teachers coming to Renton Prep, and even she herself, can experience a time of transition. This school does not give teachers a carefully laid out set of lessons and textbooks. There is a set of standards and competencies and a shared collection of commonly used content resources (Discovery Education videos, ALEKS Math, Khan Academy), but teachers are both trusted and expected to work with students in designing much of the rest. Teachers collaborate with one another and with students to design the how of learning.

In the younger grades (the Amazing Grace students), one is likely to see more of a teacher-directed approach, closer to the format of traditional schools. Yet, already in early grades, there is an intentional nurturing and preparing of students for the growing ownership, collaboration, and cocreation that is commonplace in the later grades. In fact, those who start in the school in early grades often shine in the later grades as confident speakers and in how they express their learning. This is clearly due to the intentional and important foundation building in the lower grades. Even in the younger grades, students are exposed to experiential learning, projects, and collaboration, all while getting a firm content foundation. By the time that students reach the upper grades, their time is largely occupied by experiential learning (field trips that expose students to rich culture and the arts), immersive learning in the virtual reality lab, collaboration on posters that will display student thinking and learning, and other projects. In terms of project-based learning (which is done in all grades but emphasized more in the upper grades), a student might manage two or three different projects at a time, with each project ranging from a few days to a few weeks.

Enter the school on a typical day and you will not see upper-grade students sitting in desks lined up in straight rows with a teacher at the front of the room. Instead, you will see students on the floor, creating videos, doing independent and group research, and collaborating at various stages of projects. Teachers will be sitting down with small groups of students, often working one-on-one with students more than leading large-group instruction. There will be a wide array of technologies—laptops for ongoing work and research, but also new and emerging technologies on loan or provided in beta from companies like Microsoft.

To give a sense of the stark contrast to many school environments, the director explained a recent event when a group of visitors toured Renton Prep. One of the visitors asked a group of students what subject they were learning and the students looked confused. They did not categorize what they were learning as history or literature amid a given project. To clarify, one of Renton Prep teachers reframed the question: What are you learning? Then the students quickly described the question they were exploring and precisely what they were learning.

This is not a disordered free-for-all. A clear set of competencies and standards directs student work. But the projects and ways students learn and show their learning are a steady stream of innovations. Students, especially in the upper grades, have ample voice in the how of their learning. After all, that is a core goal of Renton Prep—equipping students with a voice and set of competencies that ready them to face and solve important challenges and problems in the world. To do that, they have designed a learning environment that engages students in creative expression, research, and problem-solving.

With such a different approach to learning, it may come as no surprise that assessment is quite different as well. While the school uses occasional benchmark assessments to gauge student learning, they largely use rubrics to give rich and detailed feedback on student projects. Students will generally produce two or more artifacts or projects that relate to a given standard or competency. Feedback on those artifacts will include formative and narrative feedback as students progress through a project, but also a culminating rubric assessment that gives students more detailed insight on what they did well and areas for improvement. It is an environment where students have the ability to work and rework projects to a degree, although time limitations mean that students eventually need to call a project complete, assess the status of their work, and move on to the next project or learning experience.

Given this approach to assessment, traditional letter grades are not used at Renton Prep and Amazing Grace. Instead, reports include a list of student competencies and a rating system that includes the categories of exemplary, mastery, proficient, developing, and unsatisfactory. This language better represents their philosophy of mentoring and progress toward mastery, not simply doing work to earn a particular grade.

Yet much of the world outside of Renton Prep still thinks in terms of grades. They have a simple process for converting the Renton Prep assessment language into a grade point average when a college or transfer school needs it. In this way, the school can provide a usable transcript to those who are not familiar with Renton Prep's more authentic approach to assessment and feedback.

Some might note that Renton Prep stops at tenth grade. One might think that this is because the upper grades are newer and will eventually add the last two grades, but tenth grade is actually the final year of school there. Renton Prep is truly a "prep" school, equipping students for a Washington state-specific program called Running Start. This is a dual-credit program where high school students can take an entry exam that qualifies them to start taking dual high school / college credit courses. In this case, there are three community colleges in Seattle that offer the Running Start program. Students at Renton Prep take the entry exam and, if they pass, can transfer to one of these community colleges for their junior and senior year, essentially graduating from high school at eighteen but with both a high school diploma and an associate's degree. Students who do not opt for this pathway always have the option of transferring to another high school after their tenth-grade year at Renton Prep, but the dual-credit pathway is the assumed and common direction for students.

With such an innovative and project-based approach to teaching and learning, how are students instructed in the faith? This, too, is something unusual. Yet, there are some important and consistent practices. Each Monday, students from the Renton Prep and Amazing Grace campuses come together to worship in a shared chapel service that is led by the ordained minister or one of the two commissioned ministers on staff. Also, while the school does not have a course called "religion," they are nonetheless thoughtful and intentional about faith formation, opting for the use of nongraded, discussion-based Bible studies with all students. Yet, this, like everything else at Renton Prep, is in constant review, and they are ready to adjust the practices based on what they see or don't see in students. For example, a conversation recently surfaced about whether students had a solid enough introduction to Lutheran theology, prompting a semester-long study of the 2017 edition of Martin Luther's Small Catechism. If the school sees that students need more of something, their environment is flexible enough to reorganize to create space for what is needed.

Beyond this, there is a strong commitment to an overall positive Christian environment. The school places a high priority on teachers who share their faith openly and clearly as part of their day. There are prayer partners and cross-age mentoring in the faith. They also seek out ways to explore matters of faith through projects and other parts of the student learning experience.

While this approach may seem unfamiliar, the Renton Prep context requires something different from traditional course-based study. At the time of the last interview, Renton Prep and Amazing Grace collectively represented a combined school of over 220 students, including students from twenty-five different ethnic groups, many of whom are expatriates or new immigrants from places like Vietnam, the Philippines, Slovakia, Russia, various parts of Africa, and more. Many students come from bilingual families and a wide array of religious backgrounds. Renton Prep is clear about their Christian identity and mission, but that is not the main reason many send their kids to the school. It is an incredible mission field right at the school's doorstep. This incredibly diverse audience is part of what drives the faculty and leadership to prayerfully consider the best ways to be a clear, loving, and faithful Christian witness. They take this calling and responsibility seriously.

At the same time, this is not the perfect school for every interested student, and the admission process reflects that. Interested families might begin by filling out an application on the website and meeting with someone from the school for a time to share and answer questions. After that comes a school tour and an interview with the parents/guardians and the prospective student. In that meeting, the administrator carefully assesses parents and student. The goal is to understand how the child thinks, approaches challenges, approaches learning, and responds when the administrator throws a wrench into a simple task. There is also observation of how the parents react. Do they allow the child to make mistakes and learn from those mistakes? All of this is part of a careful discernment process to see if this student and family is likely a good match for this distinct approach to teaching and learning. It is important to see that the child is motivated and wants to be there, and that the parent will let the child struggle to learn.

All of this is important because experience has taught the leadership that, even with motivation and this sought-after disposition, it usually takes students coming from a more traditional school about three to four months to make the transition into the Renton Prep or Amazing Grace school culture and approach to learning. This is quite consistent with the researcher's study of other student-centered and project-based schools. The process of helping students build the competence and confidence to take ownership in their learning and to find their voice is not something that can be rushed. It takes time, mentoring, and a positive and nurturing community; Renton Prep is committed to all three.

When it comes to the church and school relationship, the lead administrator of the two schools is also the sole pastor of the church. This is an older congregation that, at the time of writing, worships around fifteen people on a given Sunday. The members are fully supportive of the school and see it as their one mission. Yet, while there is support of the ministry, it is not necessarily financial. In fact, the support now goes in the other direction, with the school covering the cost for the church facilities and other expenses associated with operating the church.

For many who read this story, it is indeed one of the more innovative and distinct models, at least in the world of Lutheran education. Yet, at its heart, it is a Lutheran school. Its mission is quite similar to many other Lutheran schools. The passion for ministry, especially among the leaders, is unswerving. Amazing Grace and Renton Prep are committed to sharing the love of God in Jesus Christ. While their church and school are in a region known for low percentages of Christians, they use their educational philosophy to reach the community and then use the opportunity to teach students the Christian faith through Lutheran teaching. These schools are a powerful witness to families from around the world.

GOALS AND DESIRED OUTCOMES

The goals of Amazing Grace (kindergarten through fifth grade) and Renton Prep (sixth through tenth grades) are focused upon the longstanding legacy of Lutheran education—namely, to share the love of God in Jesus Christ with the next generation of children and their families. Yet, within this school, that vision is also combined with a commitment to do so in a context where young people "learn to use their voice to contribute solutions to the challenges of our global community." Taking a mission statement like that seriously calls for careful consideration of what we teach, how we teach, and the type of learning community that we nurture. This is a driving force behind the ongoing innovation of teaching and learning at Renton Prep.

RESULTS AND OUTCOMES

As shown throughout the chapter, Amazing Grace and Renton Prep strive for constant innovation. Ask the teachers and leadership, and they will not claim to have arrived at some final destination. They are a community of curiosity, learning, and innovation. They have a steady set of content standards and competencies for each grade and from one year to the next (drawn largely from the Core Knowledge curriculum, the Next Generation Science Standards, the Common Core State Standards, World Language standards, and others drafted from within the school). The way they challenge students to learn and demonstrate that learning is a stream of innovations, with students often having significant voice in what they do and how they do it (especially in the upper grades). As explained by one of the teachers and leaders, "A goal is for students to begin cocreating learning and lesson plans, set goals and deadlines, and practice self-regulation."

In term of traditional outcomes, this is a school where students are clearly growing in competence and confidence, demonstrated in traditional ways (like benchmark assessments) and through authentic projects and even by students giving presentations at academic conferences typically reserved for veteran educators and university scholars. Not only that, through carefully nurtured relationships with companies like Microsoft and even a partnership with a Czech virtual reality company, these students are innovating and providing feedback on products to those companies. As the school's mission statement says, students are actually helping to solve real-world problems, with the hope of equipping them to take on even grander challenges long after they leave the school.

LESSONS FROM AMAZING GRACE AND RENTON PREP

As with the other cases and stories in this book, there are many potential lessons that we can learn, but we will focus upon those lessons associated with the distinctive attributes of a school like Renton Prep and Amazing Grace.

Matching the Mission and Methods

A mission statement is a written summary of a school's purpose or aims. As such, its intent is to help direct what a school does. For example, if I am on a mission to cure cancer, then you would expect me to be engaging in activities that somehow relate to the cure of cancer. If I spent all of my time playing basketball, you might question if the cure of cancer is truly my driving mission. This same concept applies to schools. If you carefully examine school mission statements and then look at the activities of the school, there is not always a strong alignment. The school claims to have a particular mission, but the methods and activities of the school do not seem to support progress toward such a mission. Renton Prep is a good example of a school that has a distinct mission—to prepare students to find their voice and solve problems. It follows that the school would ask the difficult question of what it needs to do and how it needs to do it to pursue this mission. For the leaders and teachers at the school, it led them to rethink teaching and learning, and they are ready to defend their decisions, explaining how traditional methods might not be nearly as useful in accomplishing such a mission.

A Culture of Cocreation

Agency and ownership are powerful tools for motivating people. At Renton Prep, there is an intentional effort to invite teachers into the creative process of teaching and learning; teachers then invite students to cocreate projects and learning activities. Teaching and learning is not something done to students but done with students. In this way, the teachers and students have a sense of agency as they create together. To what extent might this be useful in your school context?

The Combination of Structure and Freedom

The Renton Prep school culture values creative freedom and the ability to experiment. They do not experiment on students—far from it. They do invite students into research and experimentation as part of their learning. Without structure, this could easily turn into random activities, conjuring fear, frustration, and a poor school climate. Yet part of what prevents that is that this student-focused research happens within established and agreed upon boundaries. There might not be traditional subjects and courses in some grades and areas, but there are listed competencies and standards that students are challenged to meet throughout the year. Progress toward meeting the standards and clear communication about which standards are the focus at a given time or for a particular project helps provide necessary boundaries for student and teacher. This is important to note, as some people will try to imitate highly innovative schools like Renton Prep but fail to include that important and carefully considered set of boundaries. That is rarely a recipe for success.

Authentic Assessments and Performance

The topic of assessment may not seem exciting to many educators, but it can influence a school climate and culture more than many realize. In some schools, students and teachers are more focused on the grades that students earn than how students are growing. We sometimes call that a culture of earning, in contrast to a culture of learning. It is worth reflecting on the careful thinking behind not using grades, using narrative and rubric feedback, and other aspects of the Renton Prep approach to feedback and assessment. One need not agree with every choice to see how it highlights a deeper set of goals and values. How is your assessment plan and approach affecting student beliefs, behaviors, and attitudes toward learning? What adjustments might better achieve what you hope to see in the school culture?

Breaking the Mold

Innovation, by nature, is about breaking the mold, seeking solutions and approaches not standard within a given organization or field. Renton Prep and Amazing Grace do this repeatedly and with student involvement all along the way. They are not simply looking back to past approaches in education; they are willing to start with a goal, question, or problem and more openly consider best ways to achieve the goal, answer the question, or solve the problem.

Creating Interpreters for the Rest of the World

When a school engages in such innovation, it will seem foreign to others outside of the institution. There will be no shortage of critics or simply confused people. As such, there is sometimes a need for translation, especially when students move to more traditional contexts. That is where something small like having a way to convert their grading reports into the grade point average language of other schools and organizations is useful. While we want to innovate, we don't want to make it unnecessarily difficult for learners to tell their story beyond the walls of the school. Some translation efforts are needed, at least until the rest of the world catches up or comes to familiarize itself with the practice or approach.

They Don't Do Everything

What students accomplish at Renton Prep and Amazing Grace and how they show their learning is a remarkable thing for many to witness. However, it is equally valuable to recognize that there are plenty of things that the schools intentionally choose not to do, allowing them to be excellent at others. This has an impact on the students drawn to the school as well. For example, you will not find a list of after-school athletic programs. Students learn dance and the arts as part of their curricular experience, but after-school teams are not a focus. This is an important and valuable lesson for schools: cultivating excellence in some areas also means choosing carefully what not to do.

Finding Teachers Who Match the Mission and Philosophy

Another challenge of being a truly innovative and distinct school, especially one that is also distinctly Lutheran, is that it can be quite difficult to find teachers who are equipped and willing to be full participants in the school. Renton Prep is the first to recognize this challenge and continues to grapple with the best way to address it. They find that it is incredibly important to have a strong onboarding and enculturation process for new teachers as well as new students.

Succession Planning and the Innovative School

There is much to commend and share about Renton Prep, but a school like this often has a very important consideration. The school's original vision and leadership resides with founding and early members of the team. These are highly respected, knowledgeable, gifted people with significant institutional knowledge as well. What happens if or when they leave? Will the vision continue? Is there a system in place that makes it likely for new leadership to take over and lead in a similar direction? This will be an essential question for Renton Prep and many other schools like it in the upcoming years. In fact, this is the true benefit of a national management model like what will be shared in chapter 9; a larger organization provides continuity and the ability not only to sustain a model like Renton Prep but to turn it into something that could be replicated in schools around the country or the world.

Strategic Partnerships

Renton Prep's partnership with companies that provide new and emerging products, help build networks and connections, and assist in amplifying the story of the school is a truly rare trait. However, it is achievable for any willing school. There is always the need to be diligent to make sure that the school is faithful to its core mission and values amid such partnerships, and Renton Prep appears to have such diligence.

Faith Formation and Grading

While this is not the only example in Lutheran education of choosing not to treat faith formation or catechesis as a typical class, or even choosing not to use grades, it is rare enough to point out as a lesson or practice that we can use to consider what is best in our given context. What model or practice of faith formation is the best fit for your school and context? Why? At minimum, this is a call to revisit or review the reasons for our models and practices.

Finding the Right Fit

More than any other school in this book, Renton Prep recognizes that its distinctions make it a better fit for some students than others. That is not a judgment on the student but a recognition that the school has a unique culture and approach; some students are ready for it while others are not. The admission process is not about getting as many students as possible but about getting to know one another and finding out whether it is a good match on both sides. While some schools like to think that they are a great fit for any student, that is rarely the case. Or if the desire is to welcome a greater variety of learners, what does that mean for the methods and resources of the school?

Building over Time

To conclude, it is helpful to recognize that Renton Prep and Amazing Grace did not create this entire set of practices and approaches in a couple of years. It grew over many years of careful consideration, deep conversation among leaders and teachers, research, adjustment, and even more research. It is a work in progress. This is true for many truly distinct schools. It is often not about changing everything overnight but about long, steady progress toward a given vision.

"A School of Truth, Beauty, and Goodness"

5

THE CLASSICAL LUTHERAN SCHOOL:

IMMANUEL LUTHERAN SCHOOL
ALEXANDRIA, VA

The Challenge and Opportunity: Declining Enrollment and a New Vision

Experiencing gradual enrollment decline over the years, the Immanuel Lutheran School student body dropped to around 50 students in 2007, even amid a gradual population increase in the city. By 2017, with a renewed and clarified vision for the school and refined marketing and branding efforts, it was a thriving school serving 160 students and finalizing a 5.5-million-dollar building project that doubled the physical size of the building, allowing them to visually represent the truth, beauty, goodness, and excellence that exemplifies the education of students at this distinctly classical Lutheran school. It is a prime example for the power of clarifying a school's core identity and vision, deepening the school's commitment to that identity and vision, and building a brand around it.

THE IMMANUEL LUTHERAN STORY

Immanuel Lutheran School is not new to Lutheran education. First established in 1870, it served families in Alexandria, Virginia, for forty years, only to close just before World War I. As World War II ended, the church purchased land, moved, and reestablished the school in 1945. Yet, it was not always focused on being a distinctly classical Lutheran school. There was no specific moment in history when the school more fully embraced this philosophy; it was a steady move in that direction, initiated by the vision of a new pastor at the congregation in 2002. During this time of reaffirming its Lutheran identity and exploring what it means to be a distinctly Lutheran school, a group from the congregation attended a conference hosted by the Consortium for Classical Lutheran Education and engaged in other more formal conversations about classical education.

Even as the school clarified and rebuilt its identity around classical Lutheran education, it also professionalized its marketing efforts to recruit new students and families. It became more methodical and proactive about marketing, hosting open houses, creating a new logo, and engaging in systematic efforts to communicate its truly distinct brand in the larger Alexandria community.

Immanuel Lutheran School is surrounded by any number of highly selective and expensive private schools, with some on the same street charging three times the tuition. In fact, there was a time in its history when Immanuel Lutheran's lower tuition rate evoked skepticism from prospective families, seeing that as potential evidence for a lower quality learning community. Eventually, the school increased its tuition, while the congregation also committed to tuition assistance so that some families (including a number of immigrant families that might be deterred by the increased tuition) could still afford and attend the school.

As of 2018, about one fourth of the students in the school came from church member families, with the rest coming from Roman Catholic and other conservative Christian families. As described by the current headmaster of the school, "We attract a conservative Christian family looking for a sincerely Christian education." These are families who do not want a public school and do not want to give up a high-quality academic learning environment, but they are drawn to a school with a clearly articulated and conservative Christian identity, even if the parents do not agree with or embrace all of the same beliefs. There are many high-quality schools in the area, even some with a classical philosophy of education. However, Immanuel Lutheran School stands as, in the words of the headmaster, "the only seriously Christian school with a classical philosophy of education." While this will not draw the interest of all families, it established Immanuel Lutheran as meeting a niche that is sought after and valued by conservative Christian families in the larger community.

Becoming a school with a classical and Lutheran philosophy that permeates the climate and curriculum is not the result of a single set of early events. It is embedded into the culture and expectations. In fact, even as the classical

Lutheran philosophy is an important distinctive of the school, its intentionality about educating students, families, and teachers is just as distinct.

This intentional communicating and educating begins with open houses for prospective families. Leadership talks openly about who they are as Lutherans and their distinct philosophy of education. There is time for parents to ask questions, tour the school, interact with teachers, and even observe a lesson to get a more concrete understanding of how a classical philosophy manifests itself in the classroom. Whenever possible, they strive for visits during the school day so that families can get a better sense of what the school's philosophy looks like in action.

If families are interested in sending a child to the school, there is also an admission meeting, often an hour or more in length, that once more includes discussion about the school's core doctrinal beliefs, curriculum, and philosophy, as well as expectations of students and families. Admission brings with it the gift of *Martin Luther's Small Catechism*, a copy of *Discover Classical Christian Education: An Essential Guide for Parents, An Introduction to Classical Education* by Dr. Christopher Perrin, and other resources that allow parents to have a growing understanding of the curriculum and philosophy underpinning it.

Drawing from a fundamental Lutheran philosophy of education that parents are the primary educators of their children, the school communicates that expectation early and works to affirm this belief. There is a regular flow of information from teachers and administrators. Each week, teachers provide a broad look at the content for the week, including dinner conversation questions intended to spark good discussion about what the children are learning. The school is intentional about creating such specific and practical ways to nurture parent engagement and involvement with the education of their children. There are also monthly parent coffee meetings that are largely discussion-based but focused upon substantive matters in the curriculum and the school philosophy.

Yet this school exists in a context where both parents are typically working outside of the home and the demands of school could just as easily prevent parents and children from enjoying quality time together. As such, the school strives to put its greatest amount of effort upon creating an excellent learning environment during the school day but not creating so much after-school programming that it leaves little time at home. This means making difficult decisions. For example, at the time of the interview with the headmaster, the school had a couple of athletic teams and an after-school chess club but might be considered light on extracurricular activities compared to other schools. This fact is a good illustration of the incredible intentionality that goes into decisions at the school, truly striving to sift all decisions through the core beliefs and philosophies that underpin everything that they do.

This intentionality extends to the hiring and professional development of teachers. In fact, the rigor and thoughtfulness that goes into teacher development is one of the most striking attributes of the school. This begins with what they look for in a teacher. As with many truly distinct schools, leadership does not leave it up to chance when it comes to hiring teaches who align with the core identity. They have a clear vision for what they are seeking in a new teacher. First, the teacher is a committed Lutheran. Second, the teacher is passionate about classical education and the liberal arts, preferably with classical education or some training in the classics. As such, teachers might come from a more varied set of educational backgrounds than at other schools, sometimes welcoming new teachers who have a strong education in the classics but who do not have a degree or higher education credential in the field of education. The ability to do this varies by state in the United States, but private schools have such liberty in the state of Virginia. Third, they look for teachers who are passionate about and committed to teaching, including important practical skills like classroom management and building meaningful relationships with students and parents.

Of course, teachers they hire may be stronger in some areas than others, but these are clear guides for the review and hiring of teachers, and such differences also contribute to a personalized professional development plan for new educators in the school. Once a teacher is on board, the professional development begins promptly. This starts with an orientation and reading core texts like John Milton Gregory's *The Seven Laws of Teaching*, *Lutheran Education: From Wittenberg to the Future* by Thomas Korcok, some philosophical writings, and classic Lutheran texts.

Immanuel Lutheran School is more committed to, focused upon, and formal about professional development than the vast majority of schools today. For example, for a school of 160 students, there is not only a headmaster but also an assistant headmaster, whose entire job is focused on curriculum, teaching excellence, and teacher mentorship. This includes weekly review and feedback of teacher lesson plans, frequent classroom observations and coaching, and scheduled and carefully planned professional development that is closely tied to the classical Lutheran philosophy of the school. Professional development entails, among other things, opportunity for teachers to visit other classical schools each year, guest experts on topics relevant to the curriculum, readings, and programming to help all teachers develop a grounding in the classical curriculum in the school. All faculty are involved in the study of math and logic, for example. In fact, the headmaster estimated about ten hours of professional development per month for each teacher. The school has guiding documents called "A Portrait of a Student" and "A Portrait of a Teacher." There is no room for lack of clarity about the vision and expectations and how they tie into the school's distinctly classical and Lutheran philosophy.

GOALS AND DESIRED OUTCOMES OF A CLASSICAL LUTHERAN SCHOOL

The goals and desired outcomes for this school, while not necessarily listed in some sort of strategic plan, are clear. Immanuel Lutheran School strives to be unashamedly Lutheran and distinctly classical as it serves and supports families through an excellent education. Contrary to some perceptions of classical education, this is not an elitist school or limited to the "honors student." They believe that an education focused upon truth, beauty, and goodness is good for all children, and they strive to create a classroom that is warm, orderly, lively, and even fun. Ultimately, their goal is to provide an excellent education and faithfulness to their Lutheran mission and identity.

RESULTS AND OUTCOMES

This school is not driven by a set of quantitative measures on a school administrator's dashboard. True to their classical and liberal arts philosophy, there is a heavy emphasis upon who they are, what they do, and why they do it. Teachers receive careful mentoring, and relationships are held in high regard, whether between students, teachers, pastors, or others in the church.

Teachers are consistently held accountable to teach from a classical Lutheran philosophy. The curriculum is unquestionably classical.

While there are different interpretations of classical education from one school to the next, it is recognizable at Immanuel Lutheran by its attention to the trivium (grammar, logic, rhetoric). Logic is an important aspect of the curriculum, starting even in sixth grade with prelogic exercises. Students start Latin in third grade. True to a distinctly Lutheran approach to classical education, there is a heavy emphasis upon music, with children singing about grammar and science, music instruction in hymnody, a unifying school-wide hymn of the week, and liturgical worship led by the pastors. Central to the curriculum is a celebration of that which is true, beautiful, and good. Some things are true for all people, all places, and all times, and those truths are learned and celebrated. Beauty is studied, celebrated, and cultivated, as is goodness. As the headmaster mused at one point in the interview, "What if more young people were able to speak beautifully, whether it was about faith, science, math, history, or literature?" That sort of vision for education is what shapes the daily activities at Immanuel Lutheran School.

Yet some want numbers and test scores as evidence that this is indeed working, even though the headmaster notes that fewer prospective families seem concerned with such questions, perhaps as classical education has expanded around the United States in recent years. Nonetheless, students do take the Northwest Evaluation Association (NWEA) MAP (Measure of Academic Progress) test annually, and they consistently score above the national average. Furthermore, students seeking admission into the more competitive private high schools in the area have good success, with some of these schools giving specific, albeit anecdotal, feedback that graduates from Immanuel Lutheran School are well prepared academically, "sailing through Latin" at the high school level.

Teachers review numeric data like results on the MAP tests and respond to any important insights, but that is not the driving force behind the curriculum. As with everything at the school, it comes back to embracing and living out its distinctly classical and Lutheran identity, and positive academic results like these test scores are seen as a pleasant byproduct.

LESSONS FROM IMMANUEL LUTHERAN SCHOOL

There are many lessons to learn from a school as deliberate about its mission as Immanuel Lutheran School. For those who are interested in better understanding what it means to be a classical Lutheran school, this is certainly a promising example from which to learn. However, lessons from this school can also apply to any Lutheran school, even if the school does not follow the classical model.

On Being Distinct and Having a Clear Identity

There are many excellent school options available for young people in communities like Alexandria. One way to approach this is to see the other schools as competition, seeking ways to demonstrate one's superiority to the next school. In some contexts, this results in an educational equivalent of "keeping up with the Joneses." Unfortunately, in some cases, this results in technological, extracurricular, and other investments that may or may not enhance student learning or the academic experience.

Immanuel Lutheran School demonstrates a qualitatively different approach to this matter. They begin with questions of identity and philosophy. What does it mean to be a Lutheran school? What philosophy and approach to education best aligns with that Lutheran identity? From there, they continue to work on exploring together what this means and the real and practical implications for the school.

There is always the chance of going through such an exercise only to find that nobody in the community resonates with such an identity and mission. However, in many cases, as with this particular one, being distinct and having a clear identity and philosophy makes it easier to communicate your value to people outside of the community. While not every person will be drawn to a particular philosophy, some people will, and that is often enough to create a solid and viable school community, as illustrated in this case. The reality is that no one school identity will resonate with everyone. Lacking a clear and authentic identity, on the other hand, makes it difficult to tell your story or make promises that you can keep to prospective and current families. Some boast of their ability to be "all things to all people," but in practice, this can just as easily turn into not building a strong connection with any group of people.

You Have to Do More Than Build It

Even when Immanuel Lutheran reaffirmed its Lutheran identity and began to establish itself as a classical school, enrollment did not change overnight. Enrollment growth required intentional efforts to build a brand that is known, recognized, and respected among people in the community. It called for professional expertise in marketing and recruitment. As such, even as a relatively small school, they also have a dedicated Director of Advancement; they also draw from the expertise of board members and others in the church.

Sometimes schools do the hard work of establishing a clear identity and focus, hoping that this will garner the attention of the community. Yet that is rarely enough. Without a formal plan and effort to recruit and make the school story known in the community, it may well remain the community's best-kept secret, resulting in underenrollment and persistent financial struggles. Immanuel Lutheran School wisely avoided that mistake, investing the time and money to create and implement a formal recruitment strategy.

The Strainer

Having a clear identity calls for consistently making decisions in line with that identity. That means sometimes passing on seemingly good ideas for the sake of that identity. It means making difficult decisions. It is a matter of what we choose not to do as much as what we choose to do. The decision at Immanuel Lutheran School to do less extracurricular and after-school programming is an example of this. That may or may not be the right call in every context, but it aligns closely with their commitment to supporting strong families, and it is a decision informed by an understanding of the challenges of families in that context. Similarly, Immanuel does not have a formal technology or computer education curriculum in an era when many other schools are investing additional resources in that area. Yet they do so for carefully considered and clearly communicated reasons. They have a compelling answer for anyone who might ask about this.

These represent what can be referred to as a philosophical strainer. Schools with a focused and clear identity must strain ideas and possibilities, whether in curricular, extracurricular, marketing, recruiting, or any other aspect of the school. The strainer helps the school to remain focused on what is most important to the community and to avoid chasing after good ideas that would not support the school's more important mission.

Relationship with the Pastor and Congregation

In contemporary Lutheran education, there are varying viewpoints about and models for a relationship between the school and church. This school maintains a strong relationship with the church. It is part of the larger church budget. The pastors are both deeply engaged in the school, teaching theology to many of the students and leading all of the school chapels. The congregation, at the time of writing this, devoted over $100,000 for tuition assistance and led the charge for the multi-million-dollar school expansion project. All of these point to the fact that the senior pastor supports the school and sees it as an important ministry of the church, as do the members. In addition to providing financial support, members of the church also consistently contribute their professional expertise in various areas. This is a promising model of a strong, close, and positive church-school relationship in an age when other Lutheran schools are lobbying for greater independence or separation from the congregation. While there may be multiple models that work in different contexts, this example certainly demonstrates that a traditional church-school relationship remains a promising, beneficial, and viable model for Lutheran schools.

Intentional Professional Development for Teachers

If you want to be distinct, then you must also be intentional. Consider the time, attention, and resources devoted to professional development for teachers in this school. They have a clear and documented profile of what they are looking for in teachers, and that guides hiring decisions. When a teacher is hired, they provide books and resources to help orient the teacher. There is ongoing accountability for living out a classical and Lutheran philosophy of education through the weekly review of lesson plans. In fact, even the two pastors at the church who teach theology in the school receive the same guidance and feedback on their lesson plans. The classroom observations allow for further accountability. They have a formal program and plan that allows teachers to visit other and similar schools. Teachers also learn about topics like logic and Latin because that is part of what is expected of the students.

Having a clear identity and focus calls for this sort of ongoing and intentional investment.

Guiding Documents

As a classical school, Immanuel already has high regard for the role of text in education, but this school also carefully curates reading lists and resources for students, parents, and teachers. These guiding documents serve as sources of common ground for members of the learning community. Use of such core documents and frequent reference to them is a common trait of schools with a strong culture and identity.

The Intersection of Theology and Pedagogy

Not everyone who reads this case will be familiar with or perhaps even open to considering a classical philosophy of Lutheran education. Others will make a compelling argument that a classical philosophy of education aligns far more closely with Lutheran theology than do progressivism, perennialism, existentialism, behaviorism, or other philosophies in modern education. Regardless, advocates of classical Lutheran education offer an important question for all Lutheran schools and educators: How does our theology inform our pedagogy? If we are going to remain faithful to our Lutheran identity, then this question will be central, commonplace, and persistent in a Lutheran school. Immanuel Lutheran School certainly models that.

Networking and Collaborating

Schools with a distinct focus, like a classical school, rarely exist in isolation. They usually seek out likeminded organizations and colleagues from whom they can learn and with whom they can share. In the case of Immanuel Lutheran School, the headmaster noted reaching out directly to other classical schools (Lutheran and otherwise). She also spoke to the value of connecting with the Association of Classical Christian Schools, the Consortium of Classical Lutheran Schools, the Society for Classical Learning, and online resources like the ClassicalEducator.com forum, as well as specific consultants who specialize in classical education. Note that the strongest partnerships were not necessarily nearby Lutheran schools. The affiliations are informed by shared philosophy more than by proximity, a possibility made even easier in this contemporary digital age. This philosophical affinity and collaboration is no small part of what helps such schools to grow, refine their practice, and deepen their philosophical commitments.

The Immanuel Lutheran School Difference

The central lesson from the story of Immanuel Lutheran School is one of Lutheran identity. This is a school defined by its Lutheran identity. We see this in its philosophy, its relationships with the church and pastors, its hiring practices, its curriculum, its classroom rituals and practices, and even how it communicates its identity to the larger community. It is an inspiring and hopeful story of how one school is building upon that identity to create a Lutheran school truly committed to cultivating a love for truth, beauty, and goodness in its learners.

"Pursue Your Passion"

6

THE SCHOOL WITHIN A SCHOOL:

LIGHTS ACADEMY AT LUTHERAN HIGH SCHOOL
PARKER, CO

The Challenge and Opportunity: Implementing and Executing a School within a School

Principal David Ness was frustrated. He had just lost a student to another competing Christian high school—one with much higher tuition and larger enrollment. "I want to be a doctor," the student told Ness in his exit interview. The other school offered more science courses, which would put him on the fast track toward becoming a doctor. "We didn't like that answer," recalls David Black, the director of Lights Academy at Lutheran High School (LuHi) in Parker, Colorado. "So, we got to thinking. With our limited resources, how can we design a curriculum where students still receive a wonderful liberal arts education, but can also pursue things that they are interested in?"

At Principal Ness's urging, Black launched Lights Academy for the 2014–15 school year and named it after the old Denver Lutheran High School mascot, Lights. (The Lutheran High School Association once consisted of two high schools in the Denver area, but only the high school in Parker remains today). "I wish 'Lights' was some kind of special acronym so that the name would be more easily explainable to people," says Black, "but we also liked the biblical inspiration for our students to 'let your light shine before others, so that they may see your good works and give glory to your Father who is in heaven' (Matthew 5:16) and to follow Jesus, who is 'the light of the world' (John 8:12)." The name Lights Academy would remain.

Developed to provide a platform and opportunity for a highly motivated subset of students, Lights Academy remains an integral part of the mission and ministry of LuHi. Located in one of the fastest growing counties in the

United States due to explosive growth in the technology and business industries (Charles Schwab's national headquarters is located in the region, along with five other businesses ranked in Forbes Top Fifty), LuHi's enrollment has grown dramatically in the last five years. In 2012, the school had 238 students. Today, LuHi has well over 550 students with no signs of enrollment slowing. Dan Gehrke, LuHi's executive director, notes that the region is "not even halfway built out with housing yet." In the fall of 2017, LuHi welcomed 162 freshmen from forty-four different schools (nine of which were Christian schools). The academic environment is competitive, with impressive public, private, and parochial schools vying for area resources and students from first-generation families who have recently moved to the region. LCMS families make up approximately 12 percent of the student body. LuHi's $11,000 tuition price tag may seem high, but not when compared to two other Christian high schools that charge over $20,000. In reality, says Gehrke, most families end up paying about 60 percent of the tuition after accounting for scholarships and church support.

Families send their children to LuHi for the Christ-centered education, its reputation for the positive learning experience, the relationships formed with fellow students, and the talent level of the teachers. "Our big edge is that we have almost all rock-star teachers and other schools don't," Gehrke says. "Hiring top, Christ-centered talent is one of the keys to our success." Indeed, one of LuHi's challenges is addressing what Gehrke calls the Chaos Gap—that LuHi must continue to recruit exemplary teachers to match their remarkable growth. "So far, we've been able to hire top teachers and retain them," says Gehrke.

Current and prospective parents in the area have noticed. "We get lots of 'ghost applications,'" Gehrke explains. "Families don't come to take tours and shadow visits as much as they used to, but our applications continue to skyrocket. The word is out on LuHi." Gehrke references the book *The Effortless Experience: Conquering the New Battleground for Customer Loyalty* (2013) as a corroborating explanation of the growth trends taking place at LuHi. In the book, authors Matthew Dixon, Nick Toman, and Rick DeLisi produce research that indicates that the "dazzle factor" of wooing customers is wildly overrated. Loyalty is driven by how well a company delivers on its basic promises and solves day-to-day problems, not on how spectacular its service experience might be. Most customers do not want to be wowed; they want an effortless experience. These picky customers are far more likely to punish an organization for bad service than to reward it for good service.

Lights Academy has not only helped LuHi to deliver on its promises, but it has also solved a challenge that Black and Ness first recognized several years ago. The academy has given LuHi a vehicle to encourage and enable students to pursue their personal interests and passions within a liberal arts education. They have created a school within a school and an effortless experience for parents and students alike (though Black certainly employs long hours and much effort to ensure an exemplary experience in Lights Academy).

LuHi's mission is to "nurture academic excellence and encourage growth in Christ." Of the faculty, 85 percent are LCMS trained, and 96 percent of LuHi graduates attend four-year colleges and universities across the country. One main reason for students to join an academy is to pursue their interests and passions for a particular topic or field of study. A second reason is to gain an edge in the college admissions process. LuHi encourages students to join any of their academies (Art, Business, Lights, Mission and Ministry, Music, and STEM) as noted by their theme: "Honor God, Pursue Your Passion, Serve the Community." Students receive an endorsement on their high school transcript for completing the requirements of an academy, but the benefits of participating in a school-within-a-school framework transcend the transcript.

THE LIGHTS ACADEMY STORY AND BLUEPRINT

Too many classrooms across the country have a teacher standing in front of the room trying to deliver content à la Charlie Brown's monotone teacher. Inevitably, students ask their instructor one simple but profound question: How am I going to use this in my life? An instructor who cannot answer this question confidently and substantively often loses the trust of his or her students. Students participating in Lights Academy never ask this question because they already know the answer. It's personal.

Lights Academy is designed to provide an intensive, cross-curricular learning experience that combines elements of Christian leadership, practical problem-solving, deep study and research in a student's area of interest, and real-world work experience through internships and/or service projects. This nontraditional educational experience requires students to take responsibility for their own learning, exhibit self-discipline and curiosity about their world, develop strong organizational and planning skills, and enjoy the journey of deep study and exploration of a preferred topic or interest.

Students interested in participating in Lights Academy, or any of LuHi's academies, apply at the end of their sophomore year and, if accepted, embark on a two-year program. Once they establish their personalized learning goals, students take control over the scope, pace, place, and assessment of their learning. "Lights Academy is a program that makes students rethink their whole learning process," asserts Black. "They identify what they are passionate about and how to pursue their goals and dreams." Lights Academy is not simply a variation on another school's gifted and talented program but a program for *any* student interested in pursuing his or her passion within a sixteen-person cohort. "We didn't want a program that only fit a specific type of student," Black says. As the mission of the Lights Academy articulates, the goal is a "Christ-centered, rigorous, accelerated, and personalized learning experience that will enhance student growth and uniquely prepare students for leadership and service in college and in their chosen profession." Students not only learn how to *think* but also how to *use* their gifts and talents to glorify God.

Lights Academy is made up of four components, or four Cs: coursework, collaborative community experience, cross-academy curriculum, and a capstone project. Over a two-year period, students take their Lights Academy "class" in two blocks each semester, conducting deep research and thought, making use of uninterrupted work time, and participating in off-site opportunities and extended field trip experiences. The work of the first year is much more prescriptive for students, while the second year allows them to engage in a wider variety of learning experiences. Even as Black continues to tinker with and enhance the curriculum, a typical first year in the Lights Academy might include the following:

- ◆ A Christian guest speaker series on various career insights and vocations

- ◆ A leadership book study

- ◆ Real-world simulations and problem-solving scenarios

◆ Teaching and learning about effective collaboration strategies and techniques

◆ Collaborative projects designed to address real-world challenges with a cross-disciplinary approach

◆ Creation and development of a game plan and business plan using collaborative research practice

◆ School and community service projects

◆ Development of a personal brand and mission statement

◆ Regular reflection papers and activities, ensuring ample reflection time and faith applications

◆ Learning about research—particularly how to develop good research questions and how to employ different search strategies and tools

◆ Topical and Christian leadership studies as well as current event discussions

◆ Creation and development of a smaller-scale personalized project and program tied to an academic or faith question

◆ Personalized planning process for year two of Lights Academy

◆ Online portfolio work with the following sections:

- About Me—student profile information, interests, passions, etc.

- Projects—artifacts of all their special projects throughout the course

- Personal Learning Tab—indicators of their personal learning network

- Reflections—lessons learned from their Lights Academy experiences

- Recommendations—from individuals who have examined the work or know the student through academy experiences

◆ Presenting an idea worth sharing (in the style of a TED talk)

- Innovation project

- Passion project

- Working on presentation skills—specifically hooks, story integration, delivery, and speaking clarity

- Comprehensive reading and understanding of Garr Reynolds's *Presentation Zen: Simple Ideas on Presentation Design and Delivery* (2008)

- Embedding all speech standards in the curriculum so that students do not have to take a required speech class

Year two in Lights Academy might include the following:

- A different Christian speaker series focusing on Christian leadership and followership in various walks of life

- Deep research in a guided topic of choice

- Innovation book study

- Identifying and embracing strategies for innovation

- Student interviews with professionals to learn the reality about industries of interest

- Real-world simulations and problem-solving scenarios

- Strategic development for connecting all work and project experiences to Christian faith and service

- Long-term project development and activities related to the student's interest and aptitudes (personalized)

- Online portfolio work and completion

- Various guest speakers

- Off-site visits to business leaders

◆ Embedded lessons on government and civics according to state standards (so students do not have to take required government class)

◆ Searching scholarly databases

◆ Connecting with other mentors and experts through LinkedIn

◆ Completion of the passion project, where students must employ the SCAMPER thinking technique: Substitute, Combine, Adapt, Modify, Put to another use, Eliminate, Reverse

◆ Development and completion of the capstone project, which must demonstrate a significant faith integration element and is publicly disseminated (student must have faculty advisor and outside advisor for capstone project)

Capstone project presentations can be found on YouTube (a requirement). They vary according to student interests. Looking at one recent year, capstone projects covered topics such as "The Currency of Food—Solutions for Solving World Hunger," "Military Technologies Used in Everyday Life," "The Economics of Baseball," "Why Fortune 500 Companies Are Successful," "Is Stem Cell Research Crossing the Line?," "The Secret Guide for Getting Hired," "Harmless Poltergeist or Demonic Spirit?," "Unpacking Common Core State Standards," "Teens and Restrictive Dieting: An Experiment," "Why is America Still Overseas Combating Terrorism and Is the War Necessary to Continue Fighting?," "How NASA Is Using Nanotechnology to Improve Life Support Systems of Astronauts," "How Has Lutheran High School Made an Impact on the Faith Development of Other Seniors and What Can Be Done to Make an Even Bigger Impact?," and "Why Do Movies Still Fail?" Students deliver their capstone project presentations to a captive audience, set up like a TED talk. The academy students have impressive composure, presentation skills, and expertise. In fact, many have been hired or receive job offers simply by showing prospective employers their YouTube video. Others have received scholarship offers based on their capstone project presentations.

GOALS AND DESIRED OUTCOMES
OF LIGHTS ACADEMY

Beyond the completion requirements of the academy and the culminating capstone project presentation, the desired outcomes of Lights Academy take a longer and broader view of student growth and lifelong enrichment. The academy's focus is on developing and enhancing soft skills, leadership skills, dispositions, mind-sets, and habits, all of which are generalizable and transferable to any vocation, lifelong learning, or career aspiration.

In Matthew 16:13–16, Scripture reveals a touching scene between Peter and Jesus. Jesus asked His disciples, "Who do people say that the Son of Man is?" They answered, "Some say John the Baptist, others say Elijah, and others Jeremiah or one of the prophets." Then Jesus said to them, "But who do you say that I am?" Simon Peter replied, "You are the Christ, the Son of the living God." Though we know Peter later denied Christ, he had a strong personal relationship with Jesus—so strong that the resurrected Christ came back to reassure Peter of His love and affection for His special disciple (John 21:15–19). After Jesus' ascension, Peter went on to proclaim the Gospel to countless people and suffer a martyr's death. Peter's close personal relationship with Jesus transformed his life. Relationships matter in learning too. The more personalized the project or task, the more the student will invest in his or her own learning and growth. This is a key pillar of Lights Academy. If students can pursue their personal passions and interests, they will be more engaged and self-motivated to learn.

A second key pillar of Lights Academy is for students to identify and actually use or deploy their God-given talents and strengths. In the parable of the talents (Matthew 25:14–30), the Bible teaches that we are to be good stewards of our God-given gifts and talents and to glorify Him by serving others. How sweet to hear Jesus' words: "Well done, good and faithful servant. You have been faithful over a little; I will set you over much. Enter into the joy of your master" (v. 23).

Personalized, self-directed learning is a process that molds and shapes students into lifelong learners. Lights Academy gives students a jump start in using their God-given abilities to proclaim Christ's love and name while serving in their own homes, churches, and communities.

The goals of Lights Academy are best encapsulated by the core values of the program—faith, responsibility, excellence, relevance, and fun.

Faith

- Students will analyze life, work, and research from a Christian perspective.

- Students will apply lessons learned to their faith walk and growth.

- Students will create projects, or offer solutions, that address real-world challenges and thereby provide a platform to share or give a testimony to the Christian faith.

- Students will be able to identify their God-given gifts and use them to glorify God.

Responsibility

- Students will take responsibility and ownership of their work through a personalized learning experience.

- By conducting research and exercising presentation best practices, students will improve their listening and communication skills.

- Through collaborative projects and Bible study, students will develop and nurture a spirit of generosity, team-building, and a servant leadership mind-set.

- Students will learn how to trade (prioritize), or manage, their time.

Excellence

- Students will experience a personalized, self-directed learning approach that will enhance their appetite for self-directed, life-long learning in the future.

- Students will be able to ask good research questions and practice critical interviewing skills and techniques.

- Students will learn how to revamp and improve their work.

◆ Students will learn and identify the differences between learning and achievement.

◆ Students will learn how to receive frequent and substantive feedback on their personal growth plans and projects and be able to use constructive criticism to improve their soft skills, presentation and communication skills, leadership skills, dispositions, and projects.

◆ Students will learn and partake of opportunities to support the excellence of their peers and their project developments.

Relevance

◆ Students will learn and practice skills and dispositions that are generalizable and transferable to almost every vocation, especially leadership and soft skills, which are in demand by employers and communities at large.

◆ Students will engage in projects and tackle challenges that interest them, give them purpose, or for which they have a passion.

Fun

◆ Students will find joy in exploring the world in a less-structured atmosphere, creating a collaborative environment, and tackling real-world issues and challenges.

IMPLEMENTATION, RESULTS, AND ANALYSIS

Lights Academy has been a boon to LuHi's academic programming, school culture, and its participants. The academy experience and endorsement aids students in the college admission process—they can easily demonstrate how they went above and beyond the normal high school learning experience. By customizing and personalizing the learning process, students harness their intrinsic motivation and self-direct their own learning as they engage projects of interest and real-world challenges. In addition, students might identify a career they want to pursue in college or their future. Moreover, the academy builds and shapes students into leaders—both in the present and for the future. The leadership skills are transferrable to almost any future endeavor. Lights Academy, which is intentionally designed to be a broad endeavor and appeal to any student who wants to follow his or her passion, life purpose, or cause, continues to spur the creation of other academies at LuHi—such as academies for arts, business, mission and ministry, and STEM. Lights Academy, backed by educational research, shows that a personalized and self-directed approach to learning greatly benefits students. Black receives more feedback each year from academy students who comment that they felt thoroughly prepared to thrive doing college work using their collaborative training and skill development. In short, the school-within-a-school framework is helping students learn how to think differently and lead in their various vocations.

David Black would be the first one to admit that there were some growing pains and unanticipated revelations early in the implementation of the academy. One thing he learned is that the school must identify an academy leader who is able to engage students, build relationships, teach students how to ask good questions and manage their time, and hit benchmarks. Officials at LuHi also discovered that they needed to be more flexible with student scheduling if they wanted to make it work for those interested in receiving an academy experience. The program needed more outside mentors to help oversee and supervise student development of capstone projects. Students simply did not know enough community people to ask for help, so Black is building a database of potential mentors who are willing to get involved. Fortunately for LuHi, Black is also technologically savvy. His ability to guide and direct students in a way that appears fresh, contemporary, and cutting edge turned out to be more important than originally expected. Dan Gehrke, the head of LuHi, says, "I'm not sure the program would have the same feel if Dave Black didn't have the ability to help students use modern tools to solve problems and present their projects. Portfolio presentations on websites and YouTube are a lot cooler than simply turning in a term paper." There was also some minimal tension between teachers who used a traditional teaching approach compared to pedagogy in Lights Academy. When students recognized that teachers in their other classes were just giving them fish instead of teaching them how to fish, some students commented on how much they enjoyed their own self-directed learning approach. "I have to admit," confesses Black, "I taught a different way in my traditional classes too. I had a debate with myself as to what makes for good teaching."

Black says his biggest disappointment took place at the end of the first semester of the new academy when four students dropped out, including the future school valedictorian. "Mr. Black," the student said, "I just do better when someone tells me exactly what to do, and then I go do it well." The disappointing exchange reminded Black of one of the key purposes of Lights Academy in the first place. "I remember being so sad for this student because even though he was a good learner, he had become a completely compliant learner and was already stuck in his ways at age 17." Having four students leave the academy midway through the first year of the program also demonstrated that Black needed to do a better job explaining, convincing, and letting the students feel reaffirmed about the journey and learning process, which would be very different from their traditional education courses. "Students are not used to taking responsibility for their own learning," Black points out. "They have become compliant learners over the years. Shifting the work of education back to them, having them make choices and truly own their learning is a huge challenge, but also a huge blessing and reward as they learn to embrace this lifelong learning process." Black says he now does a much better job explaining the learning process and challenges students will confront in Lights Academy as well as the long-term benefits. "I probably had an 'if you build it they will come' attitude at first," laments Black, "but now I'm far more proactive in talking about the responsibility students must take for their own learning, as well as the blessings and benefits of the program. I also try to identify students in advance who might be a good fit for the academy."

Lights Academy came about from both a need and want perspective. In order to compete for elite students with larger public schools, as well as private and parochial schools that could provide more course selections, LuHi wanted to show prospective parents that they could match, or even exceed, curriculum offerings with competitive area schools. To use a restaurant analogy, bigger schools have ten-page menus from which to choose various academic entrées. Such a large menu selection, however, can overwhelm or cause analysis paralysis for the consumer. LuHi may only offer a three-page academic menu, but one of those items on the LuHi academic menu is a five-star customer's choice guaranteed to satisfy and impress: whatever your son or daughter wants to pursue and learn more about, he or she can do that through Lights Academy. In other words, Lights Academy provides a great equalizer and ultimate elective option for smaller schools that want to claim and possess an elite academic program. A personalized, self-directed program that allows students to discover their God-given talents, purpose, and passions makes LuHi a compelling option in a competitive education market.

While Lights Academy certainly provides a game plan to compete with other elite high schools in the area, LuHi leaders also simply desire an academic program that prepares students for college and life beyond the university. One of the perceived advantages of larger high schools is that they offer more Advanced Placement (AP) courses, which certainly have their place in a rigorous high school curriculum. AP courses, however, often focus on achievement first—getting that passing score on a standardized test for college credit—and learning second. "I've never had a student tell me they missed studying or preparing for their AP test," says Black. "However, I have had many students who tell me they miss working, learning, and preparing in Lights Academy." Black also notes that the AP curriculum is not taught from a Christian perspective and that passing AP test scores (necessary to qualify for college credit) are not guaranteed.

One of the surprise blessings and benefits of Lights Academy remains its recruitment potency. Over the years, Lights Academy students have presented their capstone projects at LuHi open houses or recruitment nights. Called "Spotlight on Academies," poised and polished capstone presenters impress parents and students alike and often seal the deal for prospective families in choosing a high school. Both Gehrke and Black have found that Lights Academy connects and makes a strong impression on middle school students and their parents simply because they can see how students are able pursue their passions or interests. Lights Academy certainly fits the theology taught at LuHi—that by God's grace and inspired by His Word, everyone can be a light to the world using their God-given gifts for service in His kingdom.

LESSONS FROM LIGHTS ACADEMY

For Christian schools and leaders, there are many takeaways from Lights Academy. Here a few of the most essential:

◆ *The school-within-a-school framework is possible no matter the school size or enrollment.* Make your cohort academy a broad catch-all class so that students who have different interests and passions can all take it. You can create a special learning experience for almost anyone in your school.

◆ *Creating and implementing an endeavor like Lights Academy demonstrates that you and your school understand how students learn.* The research clearly shows that when you let students own the learning and pursue a passion in an area of interest, giftedness, or curiosity, their engagement and enthusiasm for the learning process dramatically increases. Striving to achieve is fine, but participating in a personalized, self-directed learning process will develop lifelong learning habits, leadership skills, problem-solving abilities, emotional intelligence, and soft skills that will serve students well in all vocations.

◆ *Make the daily learning process personal and relevant to each student.* The Lights Academy model will trickle down to other courses and classes. School leaders should challenge their teachers to share specific ways they are customizing each lesson plan and tapping in to each student's personal passions and interests.

◆ *Ensure that students discover and use their strengths, or unique gifts and talents, in the learning process.* Challenge your teachers to tangibly demonstrate how they are helping students identify their strengths and applying their special gifts and talents in the learning process.

◆ *By creating a school within a school, your school can compete and exceed bigger schools in academic outcomes and rigor.* Instead of worrying about how many AP courses other high schools can offer compared to your own, build a special and inclusive academy for students who wish to enhance and differentiate their learning experience in a unique way. Provide something special at your school—one student at a time. Then, tell everyone about it.

◆ *Pick a relentless and relational leader to implement your difference-making academy.* Someone will need to be thinking, measuring, and reflecting on the program constantly as well as making adjustments along the way. Find that person who is passionate about the growth and impact of the academy and who will not let the academy remain static. This leader will need to understand that there will be a constant restlessness as to whether the process is improving and determining how much students are learning and growing.

◆ *Market your special academy.* LuHi has a special "Spotlight on Academies" that features their students. Presenting capstone projects in person or on YouTube lets prospective parents and students, as well as community members at large, see emerging, talented Christian leaders.

◆ *An academy experience reveals a self-motivated, deep-thinking, high-caliber student.* Students can differentiation themselves through Lights Academy; they can link their portfolio to any job or university application.

◆ *A program like Lights Academy not only gets important community members involved in your school as guest speakers and student mentors, but it also gives your students access to experts in their fields and vocations.* The sooner students can see, use, and apply what they learn in school to address real-world challenges and situations, the sooner they will make an impact in their homes, churches, and communities today and in the future.

◆ *Make learning fun and relevant again.* A self-directed, personalized academy permits and encourages students to pursue happiness and learn about things that intrigue or stir their soul. The personalized academy model allows students to return to the joy of discovery in the learning process. The more students enjoy working at some project or cause, the more they will gain expertise, competence, and confidence in themselves and their area of interest.

◆ *Allow students to take more responsibility for their own learning.* Students who choose to participate in a school-within-a-school framework and work on their own projects or causes have more motivation to learn and less excuses not to learn.

◆ *The Lights Academy experience compels and teaches collaboration.* Whether with their teacher, capstone project mentors, classmates, guest speakers, community members, or people they interview all around the world, students in an academy cohort practice and improve their collaboration and communication skills—valuable tools much sought after in the twenty-first century.

◆ *The Lights Academy approach is inspired by God's Word and aligns with Lutheran theology and stewardship principles.* Let us not forget that God created man in His own image. He is the Creator of the universe. He only made one of each of us for all of human history—each son or daughter of God is truly special. Many classrooms today deploy a one-size-fits-all approach to learning. Lights Academy intentionally deviates from the one-size-fits-all path and is tied to the theological truth that God has gifted each student in unique ways for service in His kingdom.

◆ *Community members and prospective families will be impressed by the skills, habits, behaviors, and dispositions of Lights Academy students.* Lights Academy students have polished presentation skills, leadership practice, willingness to receive constructive feedback, impressive interviewing and communication skills, and inquisitive and reflective dispositions. They demonstrate a confidence and real-world readiness that is attractive to college recruiters, employers, and community members. These students are trained to be forward-thinking, action-oriented leaders who make a difference wherever they go and whatever they do.

◆ *Students participating in Lights Academy develop essential soft skills in areas such as communication, leadership, self-motivation, responsibility, teamwork, problem-solving, decisiveness, flexibility, negotiation, conflict resolution, emotional intelligence, and how to interact harmoniously with other people.* Not only are universities and employers looking for these skills, but our world has always needed faithful Christian leaders equipped with these kinds of competencies.

◆ *Whether you add a cohort academy to your school or not, have your students partake of a capstone project experience, where a Christian faith element must be embedded into the research, findings, and presentation.* A personalized, faith-based project will help students grow not only intellectually but also in their faith journey. They will never forget the learning process and experience.

For idealistic and pragmatic reasons, Lights Academy has found a powerful niche at LuHi. "We need to remember that God doesn't need Lutheran schools to do His work," explains Gehrke. "In many ways, our Lutheran schools are a small business that asks customers what they want." More parents desire a customized, self-directed learning experience for their children in a Christian setting, and more students want it too. The Lights Academy school-within-a-school framework is not only a great community sell but a wonderful learning experience that equips students to go and tell of Jesus wherever they are and whatever they do.

"The Exponential Power of Association"

7

The Challenge and Opportunity: Ministry in a Depressed Socioeconomic and Urban Setting

Rejoicing in the small successes is a big deal, especially for urban communities in crisis. When students come to class on time, when over 95 percent are in attendance for any particular school day, when there are no uniform violations, and when 100 percent of the students are ready to take an assessment, urban schools in ravaged socioeconomic settings should celebrate. Even better, a joyous celebration of biblical proportion should commence when students come to know Jesus as Lord and Savior. Jesus said, "There will be more joy in heaven over one sinner who repents than over ninety-nine righteous persons who need no repentance" (Luke 15:7). Several years ago during Holy Week, one LUMIN student, on his first day after transferring from a new school, kept hearing Jesus' name mentioned throughout the school day. "Hey, just who is this Jesus character anyway?" he asked. A collective celebration ensued at the next faculty meeting when the teacher shared this bellwether and joy-filled moment.

In Jesus' ministry on earth, He thrived in the little moments interacting with abused, underserved, or discarded people. Then and now, Jesus makes everyone feel big-time and special. Inspired by Him, LUMIN schools aim to do the same.

LUMIN is an association of elementary schools in southeastern Wisconsin. Five of the seven schools—Granville Lutheran, Pilgrim Lutheran, St. Martini Lutheran, Northwest Lutheran, Sherman Park Lutheran—reside in the greater

Milwaukee area. Renaissance Lutheran is located in Racine, Wisconsin, and Ascension Lutheran Christian is in Gary, Indiana. Together, LUMIN serves approximately 1,500 elementary students.

The leadership team of LUMIN believes that sharing and teaching the Gospel of Jesus Christ is *the* answer to address the problems afflicting urban settings. If urban communities are to be reclaimed and rebuilt, Christian schools and churches must play a central role. "Lives change when people see themselves through the redemptive mirror of salvation," explains Tim Young Eagle, the founding and current chairman of the LUMIN Board of Directors.

The task of rebuilding, renewing, and restoring the culture in a deprived urban center is daunting, and cities of southeastern Wisconsin are no different. Approximately two-thirds of LUMIN students do not claim a church home, and two-thirds have not been baptized. Almost 100 percent of students come from low-income families. The number of families who actually pay tuition "can be counted on one hand," says president and CEO, Richard Laabs. The Milwaukee and Racine Parental Choice programs provide vouchers for low-income families living in the Milwaukee and Racine communities. Laabs does not worry over whether the state-funded voucher program will disappear someday due to a political sea change or funding issues. "We will do this work as long as God provides the mission field for us," he says. "If God calls our resources to be invested elsewhere, we can live with that. Until then, we serve boldly and faithfully." LUMIN has been a good steward of the voucher program. "We live intentionally within the voucher," asserts Laabs. Any extra revenue LUMIN receives from foundations, donors, and other third-party funding is applied to capital projects, new program initiatives, and wraparound services. Multiple foundations provide financial support and play a critical role in advancing LUMIN's mission and strategic goals.

Many LUMIN students come from homes of single parents who live paycheck to paycheck. Many are "working poor," underemployed, and do not have the common household amenities so many take for granted. "It can be a challenge to enforce the dress code," explains Trila Pitchford, principal at Northwest Lutheran School, "when families do not have a washer and dryer or have no money to go to the local laundromat." For many LUMIN students, their main meals, or only meals, of the day come from the publicly funded meal programs.

To minister in a depressed socioeconomic urban area, one must constantly assess the community needs rather than assume to know what is best for the community. Taking time to listen shows care, compassion, and a commitment to make a real difference. Thus, LUMIN school officials continuously and regularly engage community residents. After listening and getting input from neighborhood meetings, open forums, and public gathering places, LUMIN attempts to provide resources, commodities, and programs for the community that address these needs and interests. As LUMIN officials gather input and encourage community residents to share their voice, they also seek to provide solutions and build relationships with local families, especially those who have been previously underserved. LUMIN schools are limited, of course, in what they can do to address decades of a failed war on poverty, a growing opioid crisis, a widening socioeconomic reality, the breakdown of the American family, and many other social and economic challenges. They focus on what they can do—which is to provide a safe, caring learning environment for children; close the achievement gap; and teach and share the life-changing and life-saving Gospel message of Jesus Christ.

THE LUMIN STORY AND THE POWER OF ASSOCIATION

At the turn of the twenty-first century, the sad state of education in the urban areas of Milwaukee could no longer be ignored. Too many schools were in shambles, and there seemed to be little hope for improvement. Jesus calls on His followers to be salt and light into a very dark and depraved world: "You are the light of the world. A city set on a hill cannot be hidden" (Matthew 5:14).

Thus, beginning in 2002, the Christian community began a renewed effort to reengage and confront the challenges of urban education in southeastern Wisconsin. Several Lutheran schools, as well as other private and parochial schools, had recently closed and the trend lines were all pointing downward for the few remaining. LUMIN was founded in 2002 as a 501(c)(3) nonprofit corporation and a Recognized Service Organization of the LCMS by a group of LCMS business people and professional educators deeply concerned about the decline of Lutheran education in Milwaukee's urban community.

The dream involved developing a network of high performing schools centered on academic excellence, leadership development, and teaching the Christian faith. These schools would be supported by human care and social services designed to address the numerous barriers to learning that confront urban students and families.

Under the management of LUMIN and in partnership with the South Wisconsin District of the LCMS and the Lutheran High School Association of Greater Milwaukee (LHSAGM), Concordia University School commenced operations in 2005 after Nazareth Lutheran Church and School closed their doors. Many local leaders led the charge to keep a Lutheran school embedded in the interior of the city. LCMS South Wisconsin District President Ron Meyer, Concordia University Wisconsin School of Education Dean Dr. James Juergensen, LHSAGM Executive Director Tom Buck, and ten to twelve local LCMS pastors took action to ensure that a Lutheran school would remain viable and relevant in the inner city. When Dick Laabs, an individual with a strong business background, took over in 2005, the school had only thirteen students enrolled. By the time Concordia University School opened in the fall of 2005, they had increased to seventy-two students. Slowly but surely, the school gained recognition and earned a positive reputation in a low-visibility neighborhood. (The school would eventually be renamed Granville Lutheran School.) In 2006, Northwest Lutheran School asked LUMIN for assistance as they decided to become a choice school. From that point on, LUMIN continued to grow and expand as a network of schools with the same mission and vision. Sherman Park Lutheran School joined LUMIN in 2007, St. Martini in 2009, Pilgrim in 2012, Renaissance in 2014, and Ascension in Gary, Indiana, in 2016. Pilgrim and Ascension were new schools. The other five were turnaround schools with only one decision to make: go under or join LUMIN. Numerous churches, donors, volunteers, other parochial schools, and Concordia University Wisconsin (CUW) provided supplies, events, meals, workshops, Christmas concerts, fund-raisers, elbow grease, grit, prayers, and donations to help LUMIN get off the ground and on the path toward stability and success. LUMIN remains in partnership with CUW, the Lutheran High School Association of Greater Milwaukee, and various churches of the South Wisconsin District of the LCMS to this day. These partners impart expertise, guidance, and encouragement to the operations of the schools. Nursing, education, and social work students of CUW, for example, provide support to LUMIN schools while gaining invaluable clinical and hands-on experience in urban classrooms and settings. Some CUW graduates are called to serve in permanent teaching positions at LUMIN schools. LUMIN has approximately 180 employees within its network, including a central administrative team that manages all business and academic affairs for all of the schools. LUMIN also provides a plethora of student and family support services.

GOALS AND DESIRED OUTCOMES

The Bible says, "Whatever you do, work heartily, as for the Lord and not for men, knowing that from the Lord you will receive the inheritance as your reward. You are serving the Lord Christ" (Colossians 3:23–24). The LUMIN mission statement, which members of the board of directors read and reflect upon at *each* monthly board meeting, accentuates this point: "Our purpose is to provide safe, Christian schools focused on educational success, leadership development, and spiritual growth." Each individual LUMIN school applies the mission statement to their specific context. Northwest Lutheran School's mission statement, for example, is "nurturing and equipping all children in a strong Christian and academic environment to become lifelong learners, growing in faith, capable of making responsible decisions, and servicing God and the community." If a mission statement explains *why* an organization exists, then a vision statement shows or illustrates what *mission accomplished* looks like. The vision for LUMIN has three profound goals for their students: (1) they are prepared for high school and further education; (2) they are equipped to be Christ-centered leaders in their present and future peer groups; and (3) they will not just know *about* Jesus but will *know* Him.

LUMIN schools enroll students who have been underserved or are suffering from the breakdown of the American family, poverty, high unemployment, underemployment, social injustice, gangs, drugs, trauma, and so much more. Teachers want to challenge young people academically or spiritually, but they often find that their students are simply trying to survive the week, let alone learn collaboration skills and techniques, increase their self-esteem and confidence, and embrace a growth mind-set. "We have students who come in after six years of hearing that they are dumb, they are never going to make it, that their teachers don't know how to teach them," explains Sarah Weber, principal of Sherman Park Lutheran School. "Students and families jump around from school to school, trying to find a place that can help. And in that jumping, they never catch up or even make up ground." For many students enrolling at a LUMIN school, "there is so much skill gap, not just in academics but also in character traits like hard work, perseverance, and grit. Kids have never been told that they can. And they don't believe that they can. Kids deserve teachers who care, who are willing to try, who are willing to give it their all. They deserve schools that aren't going to turn them away, teachers who believe that even if it takes ten years, they will not give up."

Inspired by Ezra 10:4—"Arise, for it is your task, and we are with you; be strong and do it"—LUMIN's six core values provide specific insight on the objectives of the organization:

1. *Lead like Jesus.*

2. *RISE UP (Respect, Integrity, Service, Empathy, Unity, and Perseverance).*

3. *Drive every child's success ... period.*

4. *Generate joy.*

5. *Value the team.*

6. *Embrace the process.*

RISE UP, their Christian character development program, creates a framework to share the Gospel so that the Holy Spirit can inspire and shape students as disciples of Christ. Each school typically spends a month and a half throughout the school year focusing on a character trait and its application. When learning the value of respect, for example, students see how to demonstrate gentleness, kindness, self-control, and patience. Some faculty members teach a twenty-minute RISE UP lesson during school assemblies or weekly chapel services as part of the school's theological curriculum. Throughout each school day, faculty and staff also look for teachable moments, offer encouragement, and "catch" students visibly demonstrating and living the particular character trait or core value in focus.

LUMIN schools also use RISE UP to engage students and staff in restorative justice practices, which encompass the building, reconciling, and valuing of relationships. One way they do this is to employ "circle time," where students gather together weekly in a circle (facing one another) to discuss various life topics, talk about current events, or simply ask questions. A teacher or facilitator might initiate the discussion with a RISE UP topic, such as courage or humility, and let students talk about how those words and concepts make them feel or define their own lives. All are encouraged to share and respect one another's insights. Most important, students are reminded, once again, that they are a child of God and that Jesus died for each one of them. His love and mercy know no bounds.

IMPLEMENTATION, RESULTS, AND ANALYSIS

LUMIN officials admit that their initiative is still a work in progress. Just as they teach their students, administrators and teachers also embrace a growth mind-set when it comes to the overall strategic vision of LUMIN. "We have not arrived or come to where we want to be—not yet anyway," shares one board member. Indeed, leadership continues to assess the needs of the community and look for ways to meet those needs directly. Academically, LUMIN schools are making solid strides in improving rigor. "We are about continuous improvement," asserts Laabs. "We don't claim to have all the answers, so we try to look at people across the country who are doing innovative things and getting it done." In the early years of LUMIN, Laabs admits that enrollment growth had a higher priority and focus than academic programming. "The emperor didn't have any clothes for a while," he says, "but now we are improving in the area of academics too." The data supports Laabs's assertion.

Although too many students are still below grade level and not proficient in areas of math and reading, LUMIN students are closing the achievement gap and measure very favorably compared to other peer schools. As the documentary *Waiting for Superman* (2010) showed so compellingly, the assumption that poor, disadvantaged neighborhoods or communities produce poor, disadvantaged schools has been refuted by research. Under the direction of Vice President of Educational Leadership Shaun Luehring, LUMIN students continue to improve and make positive gains in meeting or exceeding standards and competencies. According to the most recent STAR (Standard-ized Test for Assessment Reading) results, LUMIN schools surpass national av-erages in reading and math by 32 percent and 6 percent respectively. Pilgrim Lutheran (fourth), Northwest Lutheran (tenth), and Sherman Park Lutheran (eleventh) rank among the highest performing "80/80" schools in Milwau-kee—a total of 96 public, charter, and voucher schools in which at least 80 percent of the students are African-American and at least 80 percent of the students meet low-income guidelines. The Wisconsin Department of Public Instruction (DPI) accountability "report cards" graded two LUMIN schools as "Meets Expectations," two others as "Exceeds Expectations," and two others as "Significantly Exceeds Expectations." Moreover, the average DPI rating for all LUMIN schools is four stars on a five-star scale. Class sizes average around twenty-two students, much lower than many of the overwhelmed local public schools.

LUMIN schools are also showing remarkable progress in the areas of stu-dent wellness and spiritual growth. Overall student attendance is greater than 92 percent. Kids want to come to school. Many parents send their children to a LUMIN school first and foremost because of the safe, caring environment. A critical component of the caring environment is that LUMIN schools focus on enriching students' mental and physical health. Much like the school featured in the 2015 documentary *Paper Tigers*, LUMIN developed its own modified healthcare program under its Student and Family Services office in 2012. Dur-ing one school day in both the fall and spring, local dental associates provide dental hygienists to clean LUMIN students' teeth (and seal them if needed) as well as give referrals to dental providers for further dental work as necessary. These dental partners also provide classroom instruction on overall dental health. Other health professionals partner with LUMIN to provide free eye exams for students. Since poor vision is one of the leading causes of student struggles in the classroom, ensuring that students have good vision is one of the most common obstacles to overcome or confront in regard to student learning and success.

In addition to helping students with their eyesight, dental hygiene, and other physical needs, LUMIN schools are encouraging students to be active in their prayer and church life. Over 50 percent of LUMIN school graduates go on to attend an area Lutheran high school. Another 20 percent enroll in a non-

Lutheran, Christian high school, which means that over 70 percent of LUMIN school graduates and families affirm the value of a Christian education and want more of it during those pivotal and impressionable high school years. While reading and math test scores still need to improve, LUMIN graduates know Jesus and identify Lutheran schools as caring communities that truly nurture body, mind, and spirit.

The rise and success of LUMIN schools has occurred because of three key aspects of their ministry effort:

1. *They pay attention and listen to their community needs.*

2. *They focus relentlessly on their mission.*

3. *They have built a network or association that multiplies and leverages their ability to meet most of the needs of their community and, at the same time, creates a platform to teach God's Word and Jesus Christ triumphant.*

As mentioned previously, most LUMIN leaders freely admit that they do not have all the answers or claim to be experts at ministering in a depressed urban setting. This honesty and humility is one of their collective strengths as an organization. They do not fear the unknown. They will listen and learn from anyone. They are also not afraid to confront challenges and search for solutions. They move forward in faith. Indeed, LUMIN officials and leaders view themselves as first responders in an urban setting that is suffering and hemorrhaging in crisis. "Too many people are running the wrong way—out of urban centers," says Laabs. "We are like firefighters charging into the flames and trying to serve the people in these communities. We can't let these families and kids suffer and burn."

The desire to constantly look for ways to be a blessing and meet the needs of their community is certainly noticed and appreciated by area families. LUMIN schools offer monthly parent meetings and family events. Whether through a movie and game night, cookies with Santa, a picnic event, or some kind of family Olympic game competition, LUMIN staff members are intentional about connecting and conversing with parents at these gatherings. LUMIN teachers are also intentional about corresponding with parents as frequently as possible. Parent-teacher conferences are mandatory. If parents do not attend, LUMIN schools mandate a conference by phone. Trila Pitchford, principal at Northwest Lutheran, has an annual goal to call every one of her families (over 150 typically) during the summer. She loves to check in with the parents, let them ask questions, and end the positive phone call with a greater appreciation for the partnership they share in raising children together. "I am amazed how parents remember this phone call," she explains, "because they will mention it to me months later. They just appreciate someone taking the time to reach out and show they care." Principals, teachers, and staff intentionally design and administer frequent contact and touch points with parents throughout the year. They are visible and accessible at drop-off points and the school entrance. They hold open houses and encourage courageous conversations about community and school issues. Many principals require teachers to call their students' parents during the first month of school. The only mandate is that the phone call must be a positive, uplifting one. Establishing a caring first impression is an important building block to a fruitful relationship. Most of these parents had never received a positive or caring phone call from a school official until LUMIN came on the scene.

Based on input they receive at open houses, LUMIN establishes breakout sessions for students and holds real and courageous conversations in the classroom about difficult life issues. Moreover, LUMIN offers programs like the Share HOPE (Helping Others, Providing Encouragement) Fund, which provides financial assistance to families via small monetary gifts or interest-free micro loans. The Share HOPE Fund has helped families address homelessness, severe hunger, and medical emergencies. In addition, LUMIN offers social work and nursing internship programs, a health program taught by nursing interns, a special needs scholarship program, trauma-informed care initiatives, and other efforts to remove barriers to learning. The old cliché certainly rings true for LUMIN officials when considering the needs of their community: "People don't care how much you know until they know how much you care." Listening to the specific needs of the community is one profound way LUMIN schools continue to show they care.

The most important way one can demonstrate care is to teach God's Word and the love of Jesus Christ. LUMIN schools provide an indelible mental model for any Christian school to embrace: all children are underserved if they are denied the teaching of Jesus and the Gospel. After all, Jesus said, "Let the little children come to Me and do not hinder them, for to such belongs the kingdom of heaven" (Matthew 19:14). LUMIN leaders and teachers want their students to learn how to persevere and live with hope on a daily basis. There is no better inspiration for perseverance than Jesus, our resurrected Savior. He has forgiven our sins and gives us multiple chances in life. Jesus inspires hope, the assurance of eternal salvation, and promises never to leave our side in this life or the next.

LUMIN students are taught that Jesus permeates all aspects of their life. They learn that they are to be a good citizen and neighbor, not just because it sounds politically correct today, but because Jesus came to serve others. Teaching Jesus, God's Word, and a biblical worldview not only helps students make sense of their world but also inspires them to live with purpose. "Kids need to be able to count on someone today because so many of them don't have an adult they can count on," says one LUMIN official. "We teach them that they can count on Jesus—He is their cornerstone."

For a digital generation constantly bombarded with messages and visuals, images on school walls certainly attempt to reinforce the mission and priorities of LUMIN. At Northwestern Lutheran, for example, the three Cs—"Christ, Character, College"—are prominently featured in hallways and classrooms along with Bible verses, college pennants, and attendance celebrations. "Lift High the Cross" is painted on an entire wall in the cafeteria.

There are other ways LUMIN students see Jesus at work in their lives. During a "bridging ceremony," eighth graders took an oath to be leaders in their school. Each class member received an individual blessing from an area pastor. Baptisms, in and out of school, are celebrated. Recently, two LUMIN students unexpectedly passed away. "No one really cares about what a child's reading proficiency is when he or she dies, nor does the staff," reflects one LUMIN official. "We do ask ourselves in those moments, Did we do enough to share Jesus? That's what really matters."

Along with listening to the community and truly being dedicated to the daily implementation of the mission, the third key to the LUMIN ministry is what Cole Braun, LUMIN board member and CEO of LHSAGM, refers to as the "exponential power of association." Laabs calls it the power of "industry consolidation," or the "network." LUMIN supports its network of schools with three teams: Business Services, Educational Leadership, and Student and Family Services. The Student and Family Services, in particular, has been a key wraparound provision in addressing and removing barriers to learning. The Student and Family Services office provides the following:

◆ *Social work counseling through interns who work daily to help students with behavioral/social/emotional issues.* Students are seen on an individual or small-group basis and given strategies that help them to stay in class and focused on academics. Interns also teach character development classes, as inspired by God's Word and the life of Jesus, so students learn how to deal with difficult situations.

◆ *Professional counseling for students on a wide variety of mental health issues through partnerships with Lutheran Counseling and Family Services as well as Christian Family Counseling.* Both agencies have professional staff at each LUMIN school.

◆ *Trauma-informed care and Mandt System training.* These informed practices put building blocks in place to meet the needs of trauma-affected students and includes education for staff on how trauma affects children and their development. LUMIN schools provide basic training on best practices specifically geared toward students who experience Post Traumatic Stress Disorder (PTSD) or traumatic stress. Trauma-informed education also helps LUMIN school faculty and staff become more aware of their own ACEs (Adverse Childhood Experiences), stress, and vicarious trauma, which often comes from working with low socioeconomic urban populations. The Mandt System provides training in de-escalation techniques for schools, mental health agencies, and other organizations. The goal of Mandt System training is to get everyone in a school setting to feel cared for and safe. The foundation of the training is recognizing and developing the tools to build trusting relationships. Faculty members learn to use these tools for effective communication and conflict resolution, especially when dealing with challenging behavior. Instead of teaching behavioral modification strategies, the Mandt System trains faculty and staff members to proactively intervene to avoid problematic behavior.

◆ *Health services that inform, teach, and assist staff to serve students with chronic health conditions—such as asthma, allergies, epilepsy, diabetes, hemophilia, and sickle cell anemia—during the day.* This office also collaborates with staff, parents, medical providers, and community resources to meet the health needs of students and assist families in finding services when needed, such as finding a dentist for a child with a tooth infection or obtaining eye glasses. In addition, LUMIN officials proactively encourage good wellness with regular health education sessions, screenings, and dental cleanings and checkups.

◆ *Special education assistance.* LUMIN has hired an itinerant special education teacher who works one-on-one with students who have special needs and disabilities. A second special education teacher provides faculty and administrators with information about how to accommodate students with special needs in the classroom. Parents of students with special needs regularly receive information about community resources like speech and language clinics, tutoring centers, and advocacy groups in order to provide the maximum amount of support possible. This office is also the liaison with public school systems in order to take advantage of the services they offer to nonpublic schools (e.g., speech therapy and academic intervention).

The three areas of focus—Business Services, Educational Leadership, and Student and Family Services—are each headed by a vice president, but all departments work toward the same goals. Laabs points to the industry consolidation, or centralization of services, as the "key piece of LUMIN." According to Laabs, the challenge that many stand-alone private and parochial schools face is that they have to deal with all kinds of issues—finances, budgeting, building and grounds, marketing, strategic planning, community relationships, admissions—that many school administrators do not have the time or expertise to address. Overworked school leaders often turn to well-meaning volunteers, if they can find them, who may or may not have the expertise to deal with these issues. "All this usually happens in an environment where the finances of the related church (that owns the school) are deteriorating, and the principal, who is really trying to run a high quality operation, is constantly told to 'cut,

cut, cut,'" Laabs explains. Industry consolidation allows for a streamlined and rational organizational flowchart—"where egos do not exist and where the mission is the main thing." A network organization can also move swiftly to confront challenges and initiate solutions. "I find that other organizations envy the freedom that we work in and the structure we have created," Laabs says. In 2015, the Freidman Foundation for Education Choice recognized LUMIN as a pioneer organization in the "Emerging Field of Private School Management Organizations."

Perhaps most important, a network or association possesses the capacity to hire talented people and share resources—both financial and especially intellectual. The real benefit of industry consolidation is resource allocation—where, when, and how LUMIN can deploy its resources throughout the network. "People really underestimate the exponential power of an association," explains Braun. "Yes, you save a little on finances, but that is just the tip of the iceberg. The real power is in sharing best practices. Even incremental sharing has a multiplying effect." Braun notes that in professional development, for example, administrators and faculty have so many more experts in the field to share and implement ideas for the students' benefit. "You can get at the problems quicker and the solutions quicker." In other words, the sum is greater than the parts. The traditional model of private or parochial education can be very isolated and rely on a few people to be the experts in too many different areas beyond their strengths and training. Industry consolidation is not just about bringing two congregations or two schools together, though that could be a start. For LUMIN leaders, the network is about strategic visioning or deploying new thinking on how best to serve their community.

In addition, the network also fosters a sense that reaching and teaching in neighborhood communities is both an art and a science. The art aspect gives an organization permission to be flexible, creative, and customized in their ministry approach. Phrases like "you just got to believe," "stay true to your convictions," "make no excuses," and "do whatever it takes" may be clichés and overused, but they truly are core values and beliefs that LUMIN leadership embraces in serving their area neighborhoods.

LESSONS FROM LUMIN

LUMIN has certainly learned from many of its early mistakes. The decision to invest and focus primarily on enrollment and infrastructure development was necessary and prudent. Laabs notes, however, that the buildings and classrooms LUMIN took over were deteriorating so rapidly that they ended up costing the association much more down the road to refurbish or rebuild. Perhaps more funds could have been dedicated to building revival earlier in the LUMIN expansion. Moreover, many LUMIN founders wish they would have done a better job of communicating, listening, and creating partnerships with area congregations, pastors, and key stakeholders who felt threatened by a new model of Lutheran education that they did not completely understand. They should have spent more time explaining the goals and rationale of the initiative. LUMIN also tried to start some new schools and failed. "I wish that churches and schools that needed help would have come to us sooner," laments Laabs. "It's easier to revive a patient than to resurrect one."

Challenges for LUMIN remain. They still rely on tuition growth (supported through vouchers) for their prime funding mechanism, and enrollment has plateaued in the last few years. Class sizes, while smaller than public schools in the area, are still too large. More classroom aids would benefit student learning and growth, especially students who are several grades behind in reading and math proficiencies. More funding is needed to fully support a comprehensive special education program. LUMIN schools serve a very transient population, which makes retention arduous and long-term learning success difficult for students who move in and out of the system. A higher proportion of students suffer from ACEs or trauma and so there is greater need for teacher training in this area and more mental health professionals.

Teacher turnover and retention remain daunting challenges. The pool of willing, capable, Christ-centered teachers for economically depressed urban settings is small, while the needs and shortages are great. Northwest Lutheran School, for example, had six of their thirteen full-time teachers leave in one recent year. The work is exhausting, and teacher burnout remains a constant reality. Training and orienting new teachers each year is a costly and time-consuming endeavor. LUMIN still needs to develop a better way to track students after they graduate so that they can adjust curriculum as needed. And, of course, LUMIN schools fight issues that will not ever be completely solved in a fallen world—poverty, injustice, violence, victimization, and ambivalence, just to name a few.

Nevertheless, LUMIN leaders are optimistic about the future and confident that God is not done with them yet. As Laabs says, "We rarely use the word *success* around here, but we do say *blessed* a lot." Out of the many lessons other Christian schools and Christian leaders can learn from LUMIN, here are some of the most important:

◆ *Make intentional efforts to engage, listen, and identify the needs and desires of your community.* Go where your families and potential students are and ask them for input and feedback on what they desire in a school. Establish a sustainable engagement and feedback loop or system using informational meetings, open forums, open houses, or various community outreach events. Asking for and listening to people's opinions demonstrates that you care. Then, process ways you can meet their needs and implement solutions. Jesus often met people's presumptive needs first before He taught them what they really needed—*Him.*

◆ *Be an early disrupter and provide a Christ-centered education for all kids.* Too often constituents doubt that they can serve "those" students or in "those neighborhoods." Constantly remind and encourage your school community that we serve others because Christ first served us. Jesus died for *all* people, and He's placed these students in your midst at just the right time. Everyone can and should learn about Jesus. This truly is a matter of eternal life and death.

◆ *Ensure that your school is caring and safe.* Particularly in depressed socioeconomic urban centers, too many families have experienced violence or live in a constant state of duress and unrest. If your school has a safe, secure, and loving environment, they will notice and feel it right away and want to provide the safe haven for their children.

◆ *Identify and eliminate barriers to learning.* Most likely you, or your school, cannot removed all of the impediments to student enrollment or learning. Focus on the one or two issues that truly disrupt, or even ruin, a prosperous school learning environment. Pick barriers that are learning stoppers, but balance this approach by attacking the barriers that are doable or that you have the resources and determination to overcome. Proper nutrition, mental and physical wellness, safety, compassion, love, and care are paramount for student growth and learning. Success breeds success. By working hard to eliminate even one or two of the barriers, your school will find new ways to combat and reduce other hindrances to a positive learning environment and student learning.

◆ *Reread your organization's mission and vision statement monthly, if not more frequently.* Even the most focused leaders in ministry need to be reminded why they do what they do. Take the time for leaders, faculty, staff, volunteers, parents, donors, and anyone who is affiliated with your organization to reflect upon the reasons why you exist. Each time you lead this endeavor or exercise, unpack it a little differently. For example, spend more time analyzing and breaking down one particular word or phrase of your mission statement. Ask people to write, in their own words, what the mission or vision means to them personally and professionally and how they intend to live it daily.

◆ *Be intentional about influencing and shaping student character and leadership dispositions.* There *is* more to life than book learning. Many students living in depressed socioeconomic areas need training in character development and leadership because they often do not see this modeled at home or in their communities. Intentionally integrate character and leadership training in your school and assess student growth in these areas.

◆ *Take time to invest in partnerships with area networks—in education (all levels), business, health professions, and social services industries.* Perhaps a Concordia University is not located close by and you cannot take advantage of their nursing or medical interns as you implement your school wellness plan. Nevertheless, look to your community and be intentional in building partnerships with anyone who can help you and your mission. Always think of what you can give these organizations or businesses in return so that the relationship is mutually beneficial.

◆ *As the leader, make it your mission to keep the mission of your school as the primary focus of your employees, faculty, and staff.* Someone has to be the mission and vision keeper. The organization reflects the mind, heart, and soul of its leader. If you want to hire and supervise people who are on fire for the mission of your school, you must relentlessly model and live this mind-set and attitude. Be the first responder to any mission drift you see or sense. Just as important, keep thinking of new ways and new platforms to share and encourage others on what really matters—their relationship with Jesus Christ.

◆ *Design an administrative structure that allows your principal to focus almost exclusively on mission implementation, student learning, curriculum enhancement, and professional development.* Let the business people worry about the finances and margins. Let the wraparound services work on and reduce the barriers to learning. Let the development and advancement people concentrate on fund-raising and grant writing. Let the admissions people recruit the families to your school. Get as much as you can off the principal's plate so that he or she can focus on the really important things like faith integration, student learning, curriculum development, and the spiritual and professional growth of your teaching staff.

◆ *Adopt a flexible, nimble, pragmatic approach to school ministry.* LUMIN officials constantly state that they do not know all there is to know about urban ministry. They are continuously listening and learning from others and truly open to better ways to operate and live their mission. The priority is to provide an excellent, Christ-centered education, not to fulfill some preconceived notion of how to "do ministry."

◆ *Build a network that exponentially improves your platform and ability to meet the needs of your community so that you can share Jesus and God's Word.* Perhaps you cannot create an association as big as or exactly like LUMIN, but where and with whom can you partner or build a network? Building an association takes a determined and innovative approach to ministry—one that recognizes we are better when we get together. By God's grace, build

a broad, community-based ministry rather than only a remnant or shut-in ministry.

LUMIN continues to search for ways to improve and expand their model in other urban settings around the country. The cries for help in urban education are many, and the first responders are few. With Jesus, however, all things are possible.

"Lutheran Education on a Global Scale"

8

The Challenge and Opportunity: Changing Demographics and a New Vision

Founded in 1998, Concordia International School Shanghai is the second of three LCMS PreK–12 international schools in Asia. After extensive feasibility studies in the 1990s and careful conversations with the Chinese government, the school opened in the Pudong District of Shanghai, a portion that was largely farmland at the time but quickly developed into a hotbed for international business, with many foreign-owned businesses and a large expatriate population, making it a prime space for an international school. As many interviewees explained, it launched in an excellent location and at just the right time, something far from certain for its founders, despite extensive research and prayerful consideration.

The school began with a modest class of twenty-two students and a staff of fourteen (with no small number of these staff coming from Hong Kong International School, a well-respected international school established in 1966). Today, after just twenty years, the school enrolls over 1,250 students from more than thirty countries, offering a world-class international academic experience, daily facing the challenges and opportunities of operating an LCMS school in mainland China, graduating students who attend top colleges around the world, and providing facilities and a learning environment that challenge the quality of some higher education institutions in the United States.

The story of Concordia International School Shanghai is a prime example of the truly global impact and world-class caliber that is both possible and at

work in contemporary Lutheran education. It also gives us an opportunity to reflect on the challenges and opportunities of navigating governmental policies and regulations.

THE CONCORDIA SHANGHAI STORY

Even with extensive research and a location in a prime and growing part of Shanghai, the future of Concordia International School Shanghai (CISS) in its first years was uncertain, especially in the first five years. With a starting class of twenty-two and a staff of fourteen, as well as the costs of operating in China, this is a school that could not survive on its own. In fact, it would have closed in those first five years if it were not for the financial backing and support of Hong Kong International School, the Lutheran Church Extension Fund, and the Lutheran Church—Missouri Synod. Yet, today it is in a strong financial situation, depending upon tuition for its operating budget but having ample reserves to accommodate any annual fluctuations in student enrollment. Being a highly selective international school, tuition is quite high compared to what many expect from a Lutheran school in the United States, potentially four times the tuition one might see in a Lutheran elementary or high school in the Midwest.

Yet, even from the early scouting visits to Shanghai to explore the viability of such an endeavor, this was not solely an effort of Westerners coming to China. From the start, founders sought input from locals and hired Chinese nationals on the staff.

Similarly, the timing for this school was supported by the goals and desires of the Chinese government as well. At the time of its start, the Chinese government wanted to attract international business, and having high-quality international schools was a piece of that strategy. Large companies like General Motors and Coca-Cola set up a presence in the Pudong district in the following years. The majority of early students at the school were from Caucasian expatriate families relocating to Shanghai for business. Yet these demographics changed over time.

Today, families come to the community from different paths. There are expatriates who come with a company and stay for a few years, up to ten years or more in some cases. There are families from Taiwan, Hong Kong, or Sin-

Adapting to Changing Circumstances

While the entire world is in constant flux and change, some might argue that Shanghai represents that tenfold. Consider that CISS is in a bustling part of one of the largest cities in the world, and it was largely farm fields twenty years ago when the school started. They knew from their research that development and growth was forthcoming, but nobody could anticipate the exact nature of that development.

Even in its relatively short existence, CISS experienced a changing student and family demographic. Because of the transient nature of the expatriate community, families come and go. The demographics of students have changed and will continue to do so. That calls for changes in how they market and represent themselves to prospective students, the nature of the curriculum, and how they intentionally nurture the warm and inviting culture that is so evident.

In addition, government policy and regulations are in development as well. When CISS first established itself in China, the government provided the school with certain provisions and flexibility not afforded to other schools. This was done in part by explaining that CISS is a guest in the city. Yet, after twenty years in the city, it is hard to argue that you are still just a guest. You are a resident and obligated to abide by the rules and regulations of the municipality. Those regulations will continue to be revisited as leadership decides what they believe to be the best way forward. Some of the practices and approaches that are commonplace in a private Lutheran school in the United States will not be allowed or accepted in this context, so members of the CISS community find it necessary to be respectful and creative in how they live out their distinct mission in such a context. In some ways, as tensions around church and state ebb and flow in different states and on a national level in the United States, the lessons of schools like CISS might become even more relevant and useful for a broader array of Lutheran schools.

The fact that CISS navigates such challenges, however, is also an incredible message of hope and encouragement. This is not always easy, but it is indeed possible. Not only is it possible, it is good and important work.

Knowing Your Audience

Leaders at CISS continue to learn how best to communicate what is distinct and special about the school to the larger expatriate community. Prospective families check out the website, visit, review materials, and certainly speak with one another about their options. Many schools find it hard to look at the school from the perspective of the prospect. We talk about our schools as we think about and experience them from the inside, but that does not always translate to someone who is new to the school. Telling this story will be increasingly important now that there are a growing number of international schools available in the area. CISS has quality academics, but learning to share the incredible community and the personal care and attention given to each student will be a valuable and important part of CISS's future role in the community.

Building the Team

After multiple interviews with people who were both newer to CISS and others who were there from the earliest days, there are fascinating stories about the building of what made up the team at the time of writing this chapter. People mused about how different leaders in the school's history prioritized different traits and factors when hiring staff. Some pointed to early ideas of largely replicating the culture and attributes of Hong Kong International School. Others noted some differences in the types of teachers sought and recruited at CISS.

Even though there appears to be some changing or competing views on this over the years, there was a consistent recognition about the importance of each new staff member. Whom you choose matters. The commitment to academic excellence matters. The educational philosophy matters. The embracing of the mission matters. The evidence of a love both for teaching and for learning matters. Whether speaking with a representative from the human resource department, academic leadership, or the head of school, each could articulate with care and consistency precisely what they sought in a new team member. They were equally able to describe whether there might be room for flexibility and where compromise was not an option.

Excellence

Either you are committed to the mission or you are committed to world-class education. That is a false dichotomy in a place like CISS, where they genuinely seek out and nurture the two in concert with each other. For example, they are looking for teachers who embody the excellence already present in the school and who will deepen or amplify its cultural and missional commitments.

Building Community

Every person interviewed for this chapter mentioned something about the exceptional and close community. This included the community of parents supporting one another, even amid incredibly traumatic moments like the loss of a loved one, and the tight-knit faculty, who largely lives in walking distance of the school and close proximity to one another. Yet they also spoke to how much students loved being at school and with one another, sometimes having to be kindly escorted out at closing times.

What people do during the unscheduled times of their day can sometimes be an indication of a school's culture. In this instance, one will see people congregating to work on shared projects, enjoying one another's company, engaging in rich conversation, or voluntarily helping one another. While some staff members were incredibly busy, it was clearly a community where people enjoyed spending time together.

There were mixed viewpoints about how such a strong community emerged, but there are a few likely reasons. One is that this is a community of largely expatriates in a massive Chinese city. Some might not speak Chinese, and the school is a safe and welcoming network in such a context. Second is the fact that, at least historically, the staff lived near one another, and proximity consistently makes a difference in the nature of how people interact. Then there is the shared mission and vision. Given the school's careful attention to hiring practices, they are seeking out people who already have certain things in common. When people share traits and seek to deepen them through intentional acts and practices, you have a recipe for a strong and positive community.

Relational Ministry

Some schools in this text present a clear, distinct, and shared educational philosophy or methodology. It is something about which the school is focused and unswerving. In the researcher's larger study of schools, this could be anything from classical education to project-based learning, experiential education to direct instruction, personalized learning to game-based learning. Is there such a vision at CISS? While it might not be as explicit and codified as what is described in the chapter on the classical Lutheran school, CISS is committed to mentoring and relationships. It is a signature of what many people value and expect of themselves and their colleagues. It is more than an aspirational goal. It is easily recognizable and consistently celebrated.

A Culture That Extends beyond a Single Leader

In one of the final interviews at the school with the headmaster, we discussed observations about the different eras of leadership at the school. With each new headmaster in the school's twenty-year history, there emerged a new set of goals and priorities. One focused on hiring the best and most academically prepared teachers; another focused heavily on teachers who were closely aligned to the mission and building meaningful relationships with students. Each one worked to set an agenda and lead others in making it a reality.

This is the nature of new leadership in most, perhaps all, organizations. Yet, for a school to be stable and grow beyond the vision of a single leader, it must have more than the vision and agenda of a single leader. That is something that the headmaster communicated as part of her goal, to challenge the community to continue coming together around a vision, set of shared values, and strategy that will stand long after an individual leader is gone. This is a compelling vision for a leader and a noteworthy lesson for leaders in any Lutheran school.

Building on Success

For well over a decade, this researcher has studied hundreds of different schools, learning from some of the best and most inspiring schools in the world. Consistent among these great schools, at least at some point in their history, is a desire to build upon and share their success. Sometimes it is a desire to reach and serve new people in the current school. Sometimes it shows up in the form of sharing their story through conferences, publications, intentional mentoring of others, or creating a formal program to invite visitors to come and see what is happening. Others display a "what next" mind-set, looking to the horizon and wondering how the accomplishments, blessings, and successes can fuel new educational endeavors. CISS is such a school. This is a growing desire that shows up across members in the community. CISS is quick to recognize areas for continuous improvement and ways to build on its success to benefit and serve others.

"Lutheran Education Reimagined"

9

THE PUBLIC CHARTER SCHOOL AND WRAPAROUND SCHOOL MINISTRY:

OPEN SKY EDUCATION

ST. LOUIS, MO

The Challenge and Opportunity: Declining Enrollment and a New Vision

In the early 1970s, there were twenty-three Lutheran schools within the city limits of St. Louis, but that faded to only two by 2011. Yet, from 2013 to 2018, a completely new model resulted in four new "learning centers" that are on track to soon serve eight hundred students (95 percent of whom qualify for free or reduced lunch), providing academics, character formation, and the option of faith formation, all on one site. That sounds like a Lutheran school; however, it's a completely new model. These learning centers are a unique combination of public charter schools and, through a separate and distinct entity, before and after school Christian education programming for families who want it. For families, it's the equivalent of walking into an educational shopping mall, where learning options are accessible and affordable for all who enter.

THE OPEN SKY EDUCATION LEARNING CENTER STORY

By 2011, a once vibrant system of Lutheran schools within the city limits of St. Louis, Missouri, declined to just two schools. School buildings once bustling with students and the familiar sounds of children learning together in a distinctly Lutheran context now sat vacant, beside or attached to Lutheran congregations, some of which also struggled to keep their doors open. This

139

was not an anomaly; similar declines occurred in urban Lutheran schools around the country, from the west coast to the east coast to cities in the heartland like Chicago and Detroit. Some cities experienced greater decline than others, but on a national level, the undeniable pattern of declining enrollment in urban Lutheran schools left many troubled, uncertain about a path forward. As models of Lutheran education in middle to high income communities remained viable, our service and influence in the most populated parts of the country struggled.

Others saw hope in promising policy innovations. For example, the Milwaukee school choice pilot program was approved in 1990, and by the 2000s, Lutheran schools in Milwaukee and other parts of the city were well on their way to learning how to leverage this new public policy to bring the hope of Jesus and the opportunity for an excellent education to children whose families could no longer afford private tuition, whose communities were left without Christian education options. One such example was HOPE Christian Schools in Milwaukee, Wisconsin, formed in 2002. This publicly funded but privately delivered Lutheran school demonstrated the promise and possibility of Lutheran education in a growing context of vouchers and choice programs.

This early experiment with HOPE Christian Schools eventually led to the formation of Educational Enterprises, Inc., later renamed Open Sky Education to better represent its expansive vision for influencing the education landscape across the United States. While the initial vision with HOPE schools in Milwaukee entailed a distinctly Lutheran school that functioned with public funding through the voucher program, Open Sky Education ventured into other parts of the country, exploring innovative ways to effect positive change in education at large while remaining faithful to their core pillars of world-class academics, character formation, and faith-based educational choices. For example, they began with an Open Sky Education learning center concept in Arizona, where they offered the pillars of academics and civic character formation through public charter schools (EAGLE College Preparatory Schools) and the pillars of Christian character and faith formation through optional Christian programming (Compass Educational Programs) before and after school for interested families.

Completely separate from the innovations and growth of Open Sky Education's efforts in different parts of the country, one of the pastors at Messiah Lutheran Church in St. Louis, Missouri, received an interesting opportunity while serving one of the many congregations in St. Louis with a vacant school building next door. Someone aspiring to launch a new public charter school approached the congregation about renting the former Lutheran school building. The pastor and congregation signed an agreement with the charter school and then created an after-school Christian ministry program for the children of interested families in that school. Some of the rent received from leasing the space to the charter school helped to offset the costs of the after-school program, making it more affordable for the children of the community to attend and more sustainable for the church to provide. Volunteers from the church and students from the nearby Concordia Seminary helped with the program, creating an incredible opportunity for the church to share its message of God's love in Christ and for people in the church to serve as positive, Christian role models and mentors for young people. It was a new and promising way to renew the church's involvement in the community and to enhance the lives of young people in the neighborhood and build meaningful connections with entire families. This after-school program, originally called The Ark, eventually had seventy-three of the ninety students from public charter school participating in the program. The church had repurposed the assets the Lord provided to provide affordable, quality education to the community through its partnership with the local charter school. At the same time, the church grew its ministry with Baptisms, families coming to church for the first time, and others returning after a long hiatus. The once vacant Lutheran school building, for some a symbol of decline and disappointment, now served as a hub for ministry and community impact and as a glimpse of what was possible in other churches and schools throughout St. Louis.

While not without its detractors, this experiment captured the intrigue of many, including leadership at the Lutheran Foundation of St. Louis. Thanks to leaders from that organization, leadership from Open Sky Education received an invitation from the mayor of St. Louis, conducting a feasibility analysis of launching additional public charter schools. By 2012, Open Sky Education hired its first regional director for the St. Louis area. In 2013, Open Sky Education opened its first learning center, including the launch of a new EAGLE College Preparatory School and also a new Compass Educational Programs in St. Louis. It continued to expand by opening its second campus in 2015, a third campus in 2016, and a fourth campus in 2017—a collection of schools and child-care programs with the capacity to serve over eight hundred students.

The public charter schools functioned as an alternative to many low-performing and unsafe neighborhood schools nearby. One interviewee shared insights from the community public schools through the perception of a Nepalese immigrant. One child sadly shared that they would rather be back in the refugee camp than in a St. Louis public school. Another child explained that the traditional neighborhood public school is where the neighborhood goes to get drugs.

EAGLE College Preparatory Schools, in contrast, quickly established a reputation for strong academics, quality and caring teachers, a record of rising test scores, safety, and civic character formation. For families opting to participate in the separate after-school Christian education program through Compass Educational Programs, parents have a safe and caring Christian community for their children in the before- and after-school hours, taught by Christians in the community.

While operating a private Christian school was a financial barrier for the Lutheran churches next door to these new EAGLE schools, they were able to fund the estimated $75 a month per student to help support the Christian wraparound ministry. As noted by one interviewee, "A congregation might not be able to fund a 1.2-million-dollar school, but it can fund a Compass program for $750 per student a year, and then maybe a summer camp for the school." At the time of writing, approximately 40 percent of the families at EAGLE schools in St. Louis send their kids to Compass programs. While that is not the 100 percent participation of a Lutheran day school, it is serving those for whom Christian education options had all but disappeared and reaching new children and families in the community.

Some might be concerned that these new public schools would siphon off students from the few strong and remaining Lutheran schools in the city. This has not been the case. Rather, these new schools and the distinct after-school Christian ministry have connected with a completely different population of families and young people, extending the impact of Christian education and Lutheran church ministry in the city.

GOALS AND DESIRED OUTCOMES

Multiple goals emerged as these schools launched and the Compass Educational Programs began. Creating a safe and excellent academic experience is certainly an important part of the effort. Yet there is also an intentional effort to invest in the local neighborhood. Central to the Compass programs is sharing the love of God in Christ with young people, nurturing Christian character, and building strong and positive relationships with the young people and their families.

RESULTS AND OUTCOMES

As of 2018, these efforts can be deemed a success in many ways. The schools are safe, academic quality is high, there is a well-qualified teaching staff, and student academic performance exceeds that of other public schools in the area. A high percentage of voluntary participation in the after-school wraparound ministry demonstrates a positive trend in that regard, not to mention the Baptisms and new church members through relationships built in the Compass programs. Many of these aspects were already described in this chapter. Yet there is another important result of these schools, even if some of the early insights are largely anecdotal.

Creating these schools is improving the quality of life in the immediate neighborhoods. The regional director explained it this way, "The neighborhood calms when you put sixty kids in an after-school program until 6:00 p.m. Most ER visits happen between the time that school is out and Mom gets home. This is a window of time where there is a higher rate of teen pregnancy, drug abuse, and more. Much happens in the vacuum, so this after-school program is making a huge impact in the community."

Beyond that, there are some signs that financers are willing to reinvest in small business within these neighborhoods. You can see new renovations of housing as well as new businesses. The narrative was once that you might get married and live in the city, but once you have kids, you move out of the city. That is beginning to change as parents see more promising and affordable quality education options like EAGLE College Preparatory Schools.

LESSONS FROM EAGLE PREP AND COMPASS EDUCATIONAL PROGRAMS

There are many promising lessons about the quality of education in EAGLE schools and Compass Educational Programs, but the focus in this particular story is the larger narrative, the story of reimagining Christian education in a context where schools are closing or closed. As such, consider the following ten lessons.

How Do I Love My Neighbors (and My Neighborhood)?

Without the willingness of a single pastor and the congregation at Messiah Lutheran Church, this city-wide ministry might never have occurred. It began with a willingness to rent out an unused building; then came the question of how to invest that money. The willingness to reach out and serve the new student population next to the church as a ministry opportunity is an important part of the founding story of EAGLE schools and Compass Educational Programs. People recalled how the pastor embraced this ministry with open arms as he greeted students and families at the school and went out of his way to make sure that families in that first, unaffiliated charter school knew that Messiah Lutheran Church cared about the community and the kids. It started with the willingness to ask a simple question, What is the best way for me to love my neighbors in a given time and place? The rest of the story, in large part, grew out of such a willingness.

New Opportunities amid Failure and Disappointment

There will always be disappointments and failed efforts in Lutheran education. As much as we might dream of a day where no Lutheran school closes, that will never happen. Lutheran schools will open and close. Efforts within our schools will succeed and fail as well. Yet the story of these schools and ministries in St. Louis remind us that we worship a God who is so much bigger than our failures and disappointments. His promises and commands are unchanging. His love for us in Christ is solid, even amid the ups and downs of life, ministry, and Lutheran education. While God does not guarantee success or turnaround stories like what you just read, they are real and possible. In fact, the Scriptures are full of such accounts, instances where God takes something unexpected and uses it to accomplish His purposes. He spoke through

Balaam's donkey. He chose young David over the older and more expected candidates for king. He took a group of enslaved people through the wilderness for forty years, delivering them to the Promised Land. He sent His Son into the world in the most miraculous way, through an unwed teenage virgin named Mary. He brought about victory over sin, death, and the devil through the suffering, death, and resurrection of His Son. Our God has a long record of bringing about His work in wonderful and unexpected ways, and we are wise to remember that fact even as we face setbacks in Lutheran education. God is good. God is faithful. God is at work today in His Church.

A Willing Coalition

As is the case for most stories in this book, this story was not the act of a solitary person. There was a congregation and one pastor. There were volunteers from that congregation and the nearby seminary. There was interest and support from an organization with resources and a shared passion for impact and ministry in the city. There was the interest and support of the mayor. Then there was the partnership with leaders of Open Sky Education, which turned out to be a key partner in making this a reality. There were likely many others as well.

This sort of broad coalition is commonplace when we see high impact and successful efforts. A good idea only goes so far. It calls for a growing coalition of people who bring together the necessary gifts and resources to make it happen. This is an important reminder for any new initiative or effort in Lutheran education, whether a new program within an existing school or an altogether new effort.

Scaling Success

There is a good chance that people in the local community could have launched a single school and wraparound ministry in St. Louis without partnering with a national entity like Open Sky Education. However, that partnership offered many strategic benefits. First, Open Sky Education, which functions in some ways like a charter school management organization (something quite common in the world of charter schools), brought a wealth of experience to this effort. They already navigated the launch of schools in multiple cities. They brought a team of experts to help with human resources, clean audits, financial management, recruitment, curriculum, training, and much more. Some tasks are best accomplished on the local level, but there is an economy of scale that comes from doing other things through a skilled and well-resourced central office. With that comes the network and shared resources of Open Sky Education schools around the country.

The Promise and Potential of Management Organizations

This important partnership is rare in contemporary Lutheran education, but it has demonstrated success in creating important efficiencies and scaling shared models or approaches in a single city or even across the nation. This story presents the idea of a management organization as a noteworthy possibility. Might the expansion of this current organization or the addition of others help to expand and amplify some of our most successful efforts and experiments in Lutheran education?

This is not only an important consideration for the local entity seeking help and support. It is also important as we think about sharing our successes with others. Why leave a local success as only a local success when it could be a blessing to people somewhere else in the world? If a central organization and entity can help us share our best stories with one another and to actually implement new efforts, it certainly seems like something to consider.

Unbundled Solutions

Starting around 2010, conversation grew around the concept of unbundled education. Consider restaurants, for example. One restaurant might have a single item on the menu, served to all who are present, whether they like it or not. No major changes or adjustments are available. You get what they serve. Another restaurant features a variety of items on the menu. They can make reasonable or minor adjustments and accommodations on the menu upon request, but your choice is generally limited to the curated selection provided on that menu. Imagine a third restaurant that serves a sort of buffet. There are dozens of different individual food items, and you are able to pick from all of those items to compose your own meal.

That last example illustrates the concept of unbundling education. We used to think of school as a preselected and served meal, with one or a few choices; now more people are looking at it more like a buffet. There are, without question, benefits and downsides to each of the three possibilities. Yet our exercise in imagining the possibilities can benefit from thinking, at least in part, about unbundling.

In some ways, we can see the distention between EAGLE public charter schools and Compass Educational Programs as a type of unbundling in Lutheran education. Some will see this model and express concern, wondering about lost opportunities for the meaningful exploration of faith and learning across the curriculum and throughout the school day. Others will look at the same thing and see a promising opportunity to fund new ministries and reach new populations previously not served in traditional Lutheran school models.

I do not argue that we choose an absolute side in this argument. We certainly turn to God's Word for wisdom on such matters, but for practices that are neither commanded nor forbidden, there is room for prayerful consideration as we think about ministry in a given time and context. In fact, this type of unbundled education thinking may well create opportunities to reach otherwise unreachable people.

Beyond All-or-Nothing Thinking

The story of these schools in St. Louis invites us to consider the value of moving beyond all-or-nothing thinking. Some see the options as either keep a school open or close it. But might there be a third, fourth, fifth, or sixth option? Maybe we rent out the building to a new charter and start a wraparound ministry. Maybe we shift to become a community resource center or a co-op program for homeschool families. Maybe some previously unconsidered but promising option will arise. The point is that Scripture does not offer us a single, prescribed way for doing Lutheran education in the twenty-first century.

Responding to Community Needs

While the benefits to the community are largely anecdotal at this time, they are nonetheless compelling. This part of the story illustrates an important lesson for any Lutheran school: all schools are placed within a given community and context, and the success of that school often depends upon the extent to which people know the school and see it as a good, important, or positive part of the community and immediate neighborhood. How is your school striving to be a good, engaged citizen or neighbor?

Voluntary Participation

Wraparound ministries like Compass Educational Programs give us an opportunity to consider the affordances and limitations of optional participation in Christian education. Honoring contemporary laws, Open Sky Education is intentional and diligent about keeping the operations of EAGLE College Preparatory Schools and Compass Educational Programs separate. The facilities are managed by Open Sky Education, and the spaces for the public charter school and the private Christian wraparound care are defined by user agreements. Of course, conversations will likely reveal that staff at EAGLE schools are generally quite positive about and supportive of what happens in the wraparound programming, but it is unquestionably distinct and separate, respecting current laws and regulations about the presence of religion in public schools.

This means that no student is required or coerced to attend the Christian programming that happens at the school building or nearby. This is evidenced by the 40 percent participation rate at the time of writing this chapter. Some will see this as a weakness or limitation of the model. Yet perhaps there are some distinct advantages to a voluntary approach to religious instruction. Consider that 40 percent of the students attending these public schools are receiving religious instruction in the wraparound programming and sharing what they are learning at home, in the school, and in the community.

Again, there are certainly benefits and downsides to such an approach, but this story gives us a chance to more carefully consider both. How could families and students within other distinctly Lutheran schools also benefit from voluntary opportunities? Might a wraparound ministry create new and promising possibilities in other contexts?

Financial and Policy Innovations

If you ask what excites someone about serving in Lutheran education, most will not say anything about finances or policy. The CPAs, CFOs, policy analysts, policymakers, and other such people might find these topics exciting, but they are not for the average Lutheran school teacher or administrator.

Yet policies can both muzzle and amplify opportunities for ministry and Lutheran education today. Being a student of public education policy can and does serve an important role as we imagine the possibilities for the future of Lutheran education, and the story in this chapter is a prime example of that. We can seek to use current policy to amplify the impact of our work and to mitigate risks, but we can also consider ways in which we as individual citizens will help influence policies in the local, county, state, and national level. These conversations matter for Lutheran education.

Similarly, financial innovations are important for the viability of Lutheran education. There are many ways to fund a Lutheran school. Sometimes changing policies affect the methods available to us, but there are always multiple ways to think about funding a single program, a school, or even an entire system or network of schools. Financial innovation is a valid and useful part of our work in Lutheran education today, and innovations in this area can have real and significant implications.

The Wraparound Ministry

As a closing thought, how might this wraparound concept apply to a current or future Lutheran education context in which you find yourself? Do you see lessons that you can apply? This is quite different from what many think of when discussing Lutheran education, but in what way does it contribute to the larger story of Lutheran education?

"Redefining the High School Experience"

10

The Challenge and Opportunity: Why the High School Experience Must Be Redefined

For Leslie Smith, head of Orange Lutheran High School in California, the crystallizing moment of her holy discontent came to fruition during an April 2014 faculty meeting. For months she had been pouring out her heart and disenchantment to her husband and administrative team on the unhealthy trends of American education and the many unintended consequences associated with it. From the outside, Orange Lutheran High School (OLu) appeared to be doing fine—more than fine, in fact. OLu's reputation as a top-flight academic and cocurricular institution was well known and embraced not only in the local community but nationally and internationally. Online and on-campus enrollment continued to steadily increase each year. Spectacular multimillion-dollar building additions and campus enhancements were being green-lit and completed. Plans for a second campus expansion were approved and set to commence. Students were excelling by every measurable category of academic and cocurricular success—ACT and SAT scores, AP scores, scholarship dollars received, admittance into elite public and private universities across the country, arts and athletic accomplishments. Smith herself was recognized as Administrator of the Year for the Pacific Southwest District of the LCMS (2013) for, among other things, her "strong Christian witness, servant heart, and exemplary leadership." Yet something continued to gnaw at Smith's conscience. OLu had a long history of winning, but winning at a game that somebody else had designed without contemplating the long-term and

151

unintended consequences. Smith became frustrated and, having served as an educator for over twenty-five years, pondered an early retirement.

Then, God provided a defining moment. As 175 members of her faculty and staff gathered for their monthly meeting in the auditorium, she asked them to stand if they agreed with the following statement: "Stress and anxiety are significant issues for our students today." All of them stood up. Next, she asked them to remain standing if they agreed with her second statement: "A significant number of our students are out of balance." Everyone remained standing. Smith recalls the pivotal moment: "I could choose an early retirement while lamenting what had become of education and the high school experience, or I could accept the challenge and determine how best to be equipped to lead change for the health and well-being of our students, our leaders for the future." God had presented a mission for Smith, and she did not hesitate to answer the call.

While Smith intuitively understood the challenges and problems that confronted her school community, she asked the hard questions and began researching the issues. Her findings revealed the depth of the problem. Indeed, she quickly discovered that students in other schools were also suffering from the obsession with elite college admission that burdened her own school community and culture. Instead of focusing on student learning, too many high schools were fixed on the development of student profiles for the college admissions process. Getting accepted into a prestigious college, one recognized by *U.S. News & World Report* in any event, superseded the joy of learning for learning's sake. Dominated by well-meaning academic counselors, too many high schools provide formulaic, cookie-cutter, one-size-fits-all advice for paths to college acceptance. Forget the learning, exploring, discovering, experimenting, and growing part of an education; an exemplary high school experience now depends almost exclusively on grade point average, class rank, test scores, achievements, résumé building, and awards. You may have heard the quote, "I have never let my schooling interfere with my education." Now it seems that students should never let their learning get in the way of a congratulatory admissions letter from Stanford or Harvard. High school has become all about enrolling at an elite university. As one OLu official put it, "It's like our students are at a lunch buffet with a huge spread and everything you can imagine there for the tasting, but instead of selecting and eating what's best for them, kids are trying to consume it all and literally eating themselves to death."

Over the years, Smith observed students living for their résumé as the college-admissions chase insidiously seeped into their minds and the hallways of her own school. When she greeted kids early in the morning, they did not respond with lively banter, eye contact, or smiles. Instead, Smith noticed that her students' "shoulders slunk, and their faces reflected not only exhaustion and sleep deprivation but bedraggled weariness replete with stress, anxiety, and depression." OLu counselors reported the emotional toll that students frequently conveyed. Cases of acute anxiety, stress, and depression incrementally increased each year. Too many parents did not see the escalation or ignored the warning signs as they focused instead on how their child could get admitted to a Top Fifty college.

The obsession with getting into a prestigious college injured not only the individual but also the school as a whole. Smith and her faculty began to notice a decline in school spirit and attendance at dances and athletic competitions, praise and prayer events, and other student activities. Students were too busy studying for hours at night, leading clubs, taking extra courses, meeting with tutors and private advisors or coaches, and completing résumé-building projects or service hours assigned to them by their crusading parents. Instead of wearing OLu Lancer gear, more students opted for college apparel even at student pep rallies, Friday night football games, or other large student gatherings. High school identity became all about the college brand.

In the chase for a prime college admission, parents were putting added psychological pressure on their child by obsessing over error-free high school "progress" and achievement. Placing perfectionistic expectations on their kid, they became even more defensive when their child suffered a setback or failure. Mistakes simply could not be tolerated—not by them, their child, or the school. Learning from failure was a lesson for somebody else's child. Their son or daughter had an elite university to get admitted to and scholarships to win. Teachers absorbed parents' wrath for their student's B or B+ test grade. How could a good Christian teacher ruin their child's future with subpar teaching?

Perhaps most troubling, the relentless mania for the golden college admission ticket—more specifically the hyperfocus on GPA, test scores, profiles, résumé building, and scholarships—negatively affected students' perspectives on learning. More students began to see their high school experience as nothing more than a series of hoops to jump through or boxes to check in order to receive the real prize—admission to a *U.S. News & World Report* Top Fifty college. College admission became more important than developing lifelong dispositions and character attributes that would serve young people well in the future. Grappling with change, struggling with cognitive dissonance, taking risks, overcoming failure, developing resilience and grit, embracing persistence, and simply taking time to enjoy the many learning moments that God presents in the most unexpected places and times were potential life lessons tossed aside. Those moments made for good Hollywood movies but not the rough and tumble real world. Getting admitted to an elite college was what would set students apart.

The drive for elite college admissions also had a negative impact on students. Care, compassion, and empathy were diminished and lacking in the minds and hearts of students playing in win-at-all-costs, narcissistic, cut-throat culture. Instead of being thankful and grateful for all that God had given them, students wanted more—needed more. Happiness became more important than kindness, status more important than sympathy and sensitivity. In short, the entire learning process had become buried in an avalanche of societal craziness and college admissions standing.

While getting admitted to a college is a challenge for many Americans, graduating from one is even tougher. Only half of the students admitted to the elite colleges in the country are graduating within *six* years. Smith and her team are convinced that the current high school design is significantly, if unintentionally, contributing to the stress and anxiety buildup in students and hindering the development of their life skills and life preparedness beyond high school. The data is on her side. Today's students are more sleep deprived, exhausted, stressed, and anxious while being less self-confident than ever before. Too many students today do not know their own strengths, passions, or life purpose; they don't take the time to cultivate lifelong skills and dispositions to aid them in the future. College counselors report that anxiety, depression, stress-related insomnia, stomachaches, alcohol consumption, substance abuse, and risky behavior are at all-time highs. Obviously, these are comprehensive issues and challenges. Nevertheless, the research indicates a strong correlation between the hyperintensive college admissions chase and culture and the emotional, physical, and psychological scars that students may accrue in such an all-consuming pursuit of an elite college admission.

Smith admits OLu's complicity in the almighty college admissions craze. "It's something we are trying to unwind because we helped cause it too," she confesses. The reality remains that OLu must compete in a consumer-driven society. Parents, especially in hypercompetitive academic settings and communities, have elevated post-high school expectations for their children. Many fear that their children will be left behind if they do not hire and spend up to $10,000 a year for private coaches, college advisors, and tutors. "Here's our reality," Smith explains. "Do you know what many of our families used to give their son or daughter for an eighth-grade graduation present? A copy of *U.S. News & World Report*'s 'Best Colleges' edition. . . . There is nothing wrong at all with attending one of the top fifty colleges in the country. We have many who do it. But do we really want *U.S. News & World Report* dictating our values?"

Smith's team acknowledges that a high school that focuses on getting their students admitted to select and elite colleges does indeed get results. OLu possesses an impressive record and reputation for helping students get into prestigious institutions of higher learning. The question, however, is not whether a school can help students get into an elite college. The real question is, At what cost?

OLu leadership realizes that in a consumer society, fear—even fear based on love—too often drives the narrative. Parents, and school officials too, fear that their children will miss out on something, not stand out in society, or not live a high quality of life if they do not go to a prestigious college. Unfortunately, this fear has driven parents, students, and schools to inadvertently teach that one is only valued by *doing* rather than *being*.

The focus on achieving high test scores and grades, receiving accolades, and gaining college admission has become more important than preparing and teaching students to be responsible, empathetic, caring leaders—to live as God's masterpieces (Ephesians 2:10). The unintended consequences of this elite college chase are staggering. "We can do better," Smith insists. "Redefining the high school experience can save our kids' lives socially, academically, psychologically, and spiritually. Their identity is in Christ, not a college admissions letter. We need to shift the focus and change the story."

FROM CREATING AN ONLINE SCHOOL
TO REDEFINING A LUTHERAN HIGH SCHOOL

There is an old saying that only Nixon could go to China. In the same manner, only an exemplary Lutheran high school could set out to redefine the high school experience. OLu has been a leader and model school in Lutheran and secular education for over a generation. A little over a decade ago, for example, OLu launched Orange Lutheran Online (OLO). This cutting-edge educational delivery system came about after leaders asked and answered the question, How can we spread the Gospel even though we are landlocked? They started the online program slowly, offering a health class in the summer. (OLu students today are required to take health class online.) They selected instructors who were not afraid to fail using a new pedagogy and developed courses based on the talent and interest of the designer.

At its peak, OLO offered over forty different courses with approximately 3,200 student seats per year. Most courses are capped at twelve students. The core courses are NCAA and UC approved, with numerous elective and dual-credit options. Courses are designed to meet iNACOL (International Association for K–12 Online Learning) standards and are taught by 120–50 professors or highly trained teachers all around the country. Online AP courses are available, and AP and honors-level courses continue to be added each year.

While OLO has approximately twenty full-time students enrolled in a given year, over 80 percent of OLu's 1,350 students take at least one online course each year. Students can take all their classes online or choose a blended schedule with a maximum of four on-campus courses and a minimum of three classes online at a lower tuition rate. OLO's format makes an OLu diploma attainable to full-time online students anywhere in the world. Since most OLO classes are accelerated eight-week semesters, full-time online students enroll in three or four courses at a time, completing seven to eight courses within a school year.

Recently, OLu added a HyFlex option to their curriculum, a very individualized and flexible education track that caters to the specific needs of each student. Students may be in class one day, learning from their peers and instructor in a face-to-face setting, and the next day they may be working on their projects on their own or online. HyFlex allows students and families to develop their own customized schedule. If students need more assistance, they can get more one-on-one time with their teacher. If they do not need extra help, they can keep moving forward at their own pace. In addition, many OLu students, as well as students around the world, use OLO courses for enrichment, acceleration, or remedial work.

Other schools took notice. After investigating the possibility of establishing their own online education program, numerous public school districts, as well as other private and parochial schools, simply have their students take OLO courses.

Time and space does not permit the opportunity to properly laud OLu for all of its academic innovation and success. From developing their own theology curriculum, which is now used by almost forty other Christian schools around the country, to the OLO program, OLu has been a good steward of God's gifts and helped many students and families grow in their faith as well as reach and fulfill their academic dreams and pursuits. Moreover, OLu has long been renowned for their athletic success and art programs, sending many student-athletes and musicians to Division I colleges on full-ride scholarships. (Since 2006, over 200 OLu athletes have signed National Letters of Intent to play at Division I schools. Approximately 750 OLu students participate in twenty-one different high school sports each year.)

Despite these impressive academic, athletic, and artistic successes, OLu is reinventing itself again—redefining what a high school experience should be—while at the top of its secular success. There are many benefits to being located in a region where many well-to-do and middle-class families can afford an exemplary private education. With these resources, however, comes extra scrutiny and parental ROI (return on investment) expectations. Paying a high tuition is acceptable as long as that high school produces significant scholarship dollars and student admission into an elite university on the back end of a high school experience. Despite these pressures and expectations, OLu leadership remains resolute in its pursuit to redefine the high school experience. "We have to make this about the students again and not the college résumés," says Smith.

GOALS AND DESIRED OUTCOMES OF REDEFINING
THE HIGH SCHOOL EXPERIENCE

The OLu mission is "to help students internalize the gospel message of salvation in Christ Jesus." Their nonnegotiable core values are biblical truth, integrity, innovation, excellence, and strong relationships. OLu's goals, values, and desired outcomes for students neatly fit a macro-framework made easier to recall with the OLu acronym:

> **One in Christ.** *Students will profess biblical truth through word and action and demonstrate a heartfelt understanding of salvation by grace alone, through faith alone, in Jesus Christ alone, according to God's Word alone. Empowered by the Holy Spirit, students will live their Christian faith and reflect God's love according to Scripture.*
>
> **Lifelong learners.** *Students will be prepared for education and life beyond high school. They will also demonstrate creativity, innovation, critical thinking, and problem-solving skills. They will be effective communicators and productive collaborators. As they continue to learn throughout life, they will make a Christ-centered impact as citizens in their homes, communities, and world.*
>
> **Utilizing our God-given gifts and talents.** *Students will be able to explore, identify, cultivate, and pursue their passions and God-given purposes during their high school years and throughout the rest of their life. They will serve others and be good stewards of their God-given gifts and God's creation. They will pursue their own physical, emotional, and psychological health so that they can serve God faithfully and productively.*

Since OLu has begun to redefine the high school experience, the leadership, faculty, and staff have crafted an even more specific and declarative statement on what defines success:

> Success is healthy, caring, strong students who understand that their identity is in Christ alone and who are prepared and strengthened for a Christian life of purpose, service through vocation, and leadership in a global society. Rather than focusing primarily on building a college résumé or profile, our focus is on preparing students for college and for life by helping them identify and develop their God-

given gifts and strengths so that they can be used wherever God calls them. The OLu Experience is a subtle shift from an emphasis on creating a profile to a focus on developing the person.

Various members of the administration, faculty, and staff put that statement into their own words:

- "We are helping/teaching students to be more selective about the smorgasbord of life."

- "We are trying to end the 'Race to Nowhere.'"

- "Our focus has shifted from outcomes to process. We are helping students learn to make informed decisions about balance."

- "Success is more about EQ [emotional intelligence] than IQ. We unintentionally taught EQ before, but now we teach it with intentionality."

- "We have to teach kids and parents to make choices and that there are trade-offs."

- "We are feeding students' minds and souls, not their egos."

- "We are much more focused on the 'Being' rather than the 'Doing' of our students."

- "It's the fight over the Golden Ticket (college admission) versus Golden Opportunities to live your life to the full."

- "Instead of preparing the path, we need to prepare the child."

- "We must have kids embrace the truth that their identity is in Christ instead of their own self-image or what the culture says it should be."

In launching the initiative to redefine the high school experience, the faculty and staff deployed a "pause.com summer"—a dedicated retreat time to reflect, analyze, and ponder anew the way things were and the way things ought to be in terms of the means, ends, and goals of the high school experience—and invested in some soul-searching discussions and self-reflection.

They dialogued on how they might implement these redefining tenets—taking the theory and turning it into practice. For example, many teachers reflected: "If I know that high school students need more sleep and a healthier life balance, why am I giving them all of this homework? How can I be more efficient in the classroom for the overall wellness of my students?" When the new school year began in the fall, the faculty surveyed students and had them keep a homework log. They were astounded by the amount of time kids spent doing homework. Knowing that research clearly demonstrated that social and emotional contentment improves and increases learning, the OLu faculty determined that two total hours of homework per night would be the acceptable norm or the goal. The faculty and administration pondered other questions: What does student of the month mean? What makes someone a valedictorian? What kind of homework are we assigning? What should "grading" look like? What are we trying to measure? Why? What kind of feedback are we giving students?

Plowing ahead like an icebreaker boat in the Arctic Ocean, Smith and her leadership team diligently worked to break through what had long been established as the norm in the college admissions hysteria of the twenty-first century. Their new strategic plan put students, not résumés, first. In putting students first, they focused on creating a pre-college culture based not solely on outputs (scores, college placements, scholarships) but also on inputs (a values-driven mission and vision, a caring culture, nurturing well-trained teachers, a safe environment that fosters community, a broad Christ-centered curriculum that includes arts and electives, an innovative approach to learning and inquiry, personalized lessons, and an emphasis on people and purpose rather than profiles, programs, and policies). Much like the father who enthusiastically and lovingly welcomed his prodigal son home, OLu prepared for the return of a healthier school culture and well-rounded students.

IMPLEMENTATION, RESULTS, AND ANALYSIS

To shift the focus and change the story of what spiritual wellness and success should really entail for high school students, Smith developed a new PIVOTAL approach to the high school experience. In each of these key areas of focus, OLu leadership designed multiple, tangible, specific changes or initiatives—many of which are countercultural in a hyperacademic environment obsessed with admission to elite universities. While space does not allow for the detailing and cataloging of all of the implementation pieces and results of OLu's ongoing high school redefining effort, here are some of the most compelling and PIVOTAL:

Purpose and Priorities

- OLu is reaffirming its commitment to making sure that students know their identity is found in Christ. OLu leaders remind students that the reason Jesus came in the first place is because they are *not* perfect or as "good" as one can be made to look on a résumé—they are sinners who make mistakes. This realization lowers student anxiety as they realize that their lives do not hinge on what they do or how polished they can make their résumés or application essays but on who they are and whose they are. Mistakes are not fatal nor are they final. With Jesus there is mercy, grace, second chances, and endless possibilities. God sees the whole person, not just the academic student, athlete, or musician. OLu students are learning to see themselves as God sees them—redeemed and loved children thanks be to Jesus, their intercessor—rather than how the world views them as a generic member of Generation Z.

- In addition to connecting students daily to Christ, OLu is prioritizing learning over grades, life over college, thriving over surviving, living life over making a living, significance over success, and character over reputation. School officials help students find colleges that are the right fit for them rather than manipulating a student's résumé to meet some college's preconceived notion of who they should be.

- The new focus has realigned faculty and staff around a common purpose and reinvigorated their ministry. They are teaching, modeling, and living out the priorities of a Christian—being rather than doing, balance, not making gods out of earthly things, and serving others before self.

- The new initiative has resonated with students and families. The vast majority are grateful and supportive of the redefining effort. While some were initially concerned that OLu would become less rigorous academically and that the number of students admitted to top colleges might decline, the opposite has actually occurred. While the redefinition is only a few years old, parents have embraced the initiative and expressed appreciation for the high school reformation and the positive, wholesome changes they are seeing in their children. OLu enrollment is rising. Relationships with partner schools have improved. Standardized ACT and AP test scores have gotten better. More students are signing up for AP courses. Even as OLu has tried to lessen the college admissions pressure cooker, the number of their graduates admitted to top-rated colleges (particularly in the Ivy League) has actually risen. Students have embraced the concept wholeheartedly. They are talking about emotional intelligence (EQ), writing about well-roundedness, and speaking about well-being and proper mental health. The focus has shifted from doing profiles for college to being a profile of courage in Christ. They are taking more time to live and enjoy an authentic high school experience.

Involved and Invested

- OLu earnestly desires that students will not only enjoy their high school experience but also be inspired to grow, learn, and discover their gifts and identity in Christ. Research indicates that associating with friends, laughing, expressing feelings, and lighthearted fun all reduce stress, which significantly aids the learning process.

- OLu recently created a Student Life Department, which intentionally integrates athletics, missions, student leadership, and the arts to create more student involvement, promote relationships, and foster fun and healthy exploration time.

- OLu created a World Council, which organizes the entire student body into seven continents and 128 smaller country groups (homerooms)—each with approximately ten students and a faculty or staff member. Each country consists of randomly assigned students from their Freshmen Ignite groups and theology classes. Country groups remain together for all four years of high school, allowing students and staff leaders to develop meaningful relationships. World Council generates a playful and lighthearted sense of fun through competitions, team discussions, intrateam-building activities, leadership lessons (OLu first used *Habitudes* developed by Dr. Tim Elmore of Growing Leaders, but they have now developed their own thematic leadership lessons and activities centered around emotional intelligence and empathy), and social emotional learning (SEL). World Council operates and is responsible for the following:

— ROAM (Revitalize on a Monday). Offered every six weeks, ROAM is designed to create space in students' busy schedules and have them participate in activities that best fit their needs. Options may include study sessions, praise and prayer, Bible study, games, tutoring, interactive activities, meetings with teachers or coaches, yoga, quiet room, making friendship bracelets, Zumba, kickball, line dancing, s'mores on Bunsen burners, pancakes, creative writing, board games, current event discussions, club meetings, walking, and comfort dogs. Faculty and staff volunteer to lead the various ROAM activities, and as many as sixty different options have been offered simultaneously.

— World Council Weeks. During these specific times, students focus on a specific leadership lesson from *Habitudes* or their own self-designed leadership curriculum. The lesson is first taught to the Student Leadership Team, and then they develop a theme week of instruction, activities, and environmental campus cues for the entire student body.

• OLu's Missions program runs five mission trips annually, with over six hundred participants visiting locations such as China, Romania, Mexico, Belize, Australia, Vietnam, Malawi, Ethiopia, India, Taiwan, South Korea, Argentina, the Dominican Republic, Cambodia, Venezuela, New Orleans, and the Appalachian Mountain region in the United States.

Values

- By themselves, hard work, achievement, and happiness seem like harmless, noble endeavors. But when they are tied only to a successful college admissions process, then they can overwhelm the development of empathy, compassion, gratitude, generosity, life balance, resiliency, grit, accountability, and keeping one's priorities centered on Christ. OLu is modeling and encouraging students that the goal in life is not just to get into a prestigious college and "be happy" but also to live a fulfilling and joyous life that helps others as inspired by Jesus and God's Word.

- Building more free or exploration time into a student's schedule, like ROAM, may look like wasted time in the go-go secular world. But research clearly indicates that a lack of downtime curbs empathy—a highly desirable characteristic for any Christian servant leader and something employers look for more and more.

- OLu has taken steps to redefine academic recognition. Now the student of the month award is based on student improvement and growth, not achievement exclusively. The Lancer Award significantly accounts for a student's EQ and SEL. OLu is finding more ways and opportunities to recognize students for their grit, resilience, perseverance, and service rather than their ACT scores, GPA, and college acceptance letters.

Optimize

- "Going to the max" on the college admissions chase puts things out of balance. Teaching students to optimize their life choices—to make their life as efficient as possible for the best results—is a life skill OLu teaches students to embrace for the rest of their lives.

- To create adaptive and personalized paths of education for future students, OLu continues to research and implement different time variables, internships, academic programs, badges, microcredentials, and delivery systems. While OLu still offers over twenty honors-level courses and nineteen

AP courses, they will be adding program offerings and specialties through certificates—learning tracks for students interested in future vocations in the culinary and hospitality field, as well as for those who have interest in becoming electricians, plumbers, or supply-chain managers.

- OLu students are taking more initiative and responsibility for their own education and leadership development, especially as teachers have embraced more self-directed and project-based learning approaches in the classroom. Curriculum and instructional leaders have been a big asset in helping teachers move past traditional sage-on-the-stage pedagogy.

- OLu has five full-time advisors, or learning coaches, to help students determine the best college fit for their God-given abilities, dreams, and long-term aspirations. OLu's commitment to keep caseloads small for advisors is intentional and rooted in their high school reformation efforts. Advisors want to have the time to coach and advocate for students on personal, social, and emotional levels.

- OLu's counseling department engages students on a redefined high school plan and emphasizes getting to know the student as a special child of God. Freshman are required to take the Myers-Briggs Type Indicator test to increase awareness of personal strengths and limitations for themselves and others. Students create goals for their college admission process on College Planning Day and continuously reevaluate these goals with their learning coach over the next four years.

- Since the launch of the redefining initiative, OLu counselors have noticed that students compare themselves less to others but engage in more talk and reflection on making a college selection that is the best fit for them.

Time

- OLu is dedicated to teaching students and families the preciousness of time and informed decision-making using a cost-benefit analysis in order to be good stewards of their time.

- Through discussions, campus events, and newsletters, OLu informs and educates students and parents on the value and importance of getting at least eight hours of sleep each night.
- In an effort to put the physical and psychological needs of the students first, OLu recently made the switch to begin school almost an hour later than it had traditionally started. School now begins at 8:25 a.m.
- OLu faculty meet by departments every Wednesday morning for Professional Learning Community (PLC) work, often focusing on how to continually improve and enhance the redefining process.

Academies

- OLu's academies—STEM, Faith and Entrepreneurial Academy (FEBA), Humanities, Arts, and Ministry—package existing courses to make a customized learning experience that allows students to pursue some of their personal interests.
- The academies are designed to inspire, strengthen, and prepare students; increase their options; and enhance their resiliency and personal accountability.

Leadership

- OLu is intentional about integrating SEL in the curriculum and helping students cultivate their EQ. Research consistently shows the singular importance of EQ in developing empathy, self-awareness, self-regulation, leadership skills, social skills, communication skills, management practices, strong and meaningful relationships, perseverance, and other essential skills for the twenty-first-century workforce.
- The leadership of OLu continuously communicates with their school community on the redefining experience. Their weekly and monthly email communications constantly reference the latest research on wellness topics. School officials, like Leslie Smith, write articles informing parents of OLu's

goals, their rationale, and results of the initiative. Open house events and parent forums, called OLuminate, are also used to communicate and dialogue with OLu constituents on their approach. OLu leadership and faculty also provide parent seminars on EQ, social and emotional issues, wellness, Christian stewardship, and other aspects of redefining the high school process.

- OLu faculty develop and maintain teacher professional growth portfolios. Among other things, teachers select one pedagogical aspect they wish to improve or enhance, submit student work they have analyzed, set SMART goals, and reflect on how they are redefining the high school experience in their own classroom and spheres of influence.

- OLu leadership celebrates alternative teaching approaches in the *Champions of Teaching and Learning* blog. Articles such as "Football and US History," "Press Conference," "War in Biology," "The Scarlet Letter," "How to Earn a Week of No Homework," "Socratic Circles," "Eclipse at OLu," "Ice Cream or Spaghetti?," "What Is That Smell?" "Carpe Diem: Seize the Games," "Let's Have S'More Chemistry: Marshmallows, Chocolate, Grams, and Moles," and "Bringing Competition into the Classroom" are just a few examples of the different courses and instructors who have been featured in the *Champions* blog.

- OLu teachers conduct peer reviews regularly, focusing on specific skills to improve or enhance.

- The OLu academic team conducts walkabouts frequently, taking time to observe colleagues, give descriptive feedback, and dialogue on educational philosophy and adjustments that might be beneficial in the redefining process.

- OLu faculty and staff have truly embraced the redefining initiative. Smith notes that her faculty is much more united, student-centered, and competent in using student data. "They are in their silos much less," she contends. "This whole changeover has been really exciting. I get a new article from a faculty member almost every week reaffirming parts of our vision" (e.g., faculty schedule, later start, importance of sleep, or self-directed learning). In almost every decision process the OLu faculty work through, they ask, What might be the unintended consequences of what we are trying to do? The learning environment is inspirational, collaborative, and mission-driven. The students are not the only ones benefiting from the high school reformation effort.

- For years during the graduation ceremony, OLu had always mentioned the graduate's name and the college or university he or she planned to attend in the fall. While the individual's name still appears on the projection screen as he or she walks across the stage, officials no longer mention the student's college choice at the ceremony. (Students can post three highlights on their slide for the projection screen—of which college choice may be one.) Each graduate is special, not because of the university he or she plans to attend in the fall, but because he or she is a child of God and redeemed by a merciful and grace-filled Savior.

LESSONS FROM OLU'S REDEFINING THE HIGH SCHOOL EXPERIENCE

Ephesians 2:8–10 reminds us that "by grace you have been saved through faith. And this is not your own doing; it is the gift of God, not a result of works, so that no one may boast. For we are His workmanship, created in Christ Jesus for good works, which God prepared beforehand, that we should walk in them." In redefining the high school experience, OLu is walking on the path that God has set before them. Challenges certainly remain. OLu must determine which longitudinal data to collect and analyze as their graduates progress through college and beyond. OLu leadership is looking for more precise wellness instruments to measure their students' social and emotional well-being. While standardized test scores, enrollment, and admission into prestigious colleges have increased since the new initiative, one may wonder if future families would stay committed to OLu if student test scores and admission into elite colleges declined in the pursuit of a more well-rounded, emotionally stable, and spiritually healthy student.

So far, however, the early results show that the redefinition experience has been a secular success and splendid spiritual reformation. While there are many takeaways for Christian schools and Christian leaders, here are a few of the most profound:

- *Call or hire a leader who ardently believes in redefining the high school experience and will be relentless in making the vision a reality.* In order to make the redefining effort a reality, CEO and executive director Todd Moritz knew that Smith needed to be free of the everyday operations of the school and academic program. Thus, Smith assumed a new position as head of school while Todd Eklund succeeded her as principal. With this new administrative structure in place, Smith could focus more on the redefining overhaul that everyone knew would take concentrated time, talent, grit, and perseverance to accomplish. "I could not lead and move this redefinition process forward without Todd Eklund's enthusiasm and belief in what we're are doing," says Smith. "He's been my right-hand man." In addition to Eklund, Smith credits Drew Heim, Kim Hahn, Rachel Eklund, Tim Detviler, Steve Barrillier, and her administrative team for getting behind the redefinition effort and staying focused on how to improve it. If it takes a team to move the mission or ball down the field, it certainly takes a quarterback to rally the team. Perhaps your school does not have the administrative resources, size, or expertise to do what OLu did. Nevertheless, if you want to redefine your school in any way, you need a movement leader. The Protestant Reformation needed a Luther. The civil rights movement need a Martin Luther King Jr. The first indicator of any level of seriousness or dedication to a movement or vision is to establish a structure or system that empowers the leader to lead. Make it happen in your context using the gifts and resources God has provided you.

- *Conduct an unvarnished cultural audit and faith audit on your school.* Smith surveyed her faculty, students, and constituents to validate her own intuition and holy discontent. You cannot redefine or change something if you do not identify the problems or obstacles that must be reformed, changed, or eradicated in your school culture. What is your holy discontent? Are you even willing to look for or admit that your school is off mission or focused on the wrong things? What are you doing about your school's malaise?

◆ *Embrace the research and plot a solution.* One reason for OLu's success is the massive amount of data and research that backed and bolstered Smith's gut feelings about the cultural challenges confronting OLu. Redefining the high school experience did not come about on a whim but from a wealth of research and, most important, reflecting on the wisdom of God. (For a Christian, conducting research always means delving deeply into the Scriptures.) With abundant research and God's Word in your backpack, it's much easier to take the first steps on a long journey for change.

◆ *Invest time in selecting precise language you want to use—metaphors, word images, and Bible verses—to educate and influence your constituents in a change initiative or redefinition process.* Smith, very adeptly and compellingly, adopted and deployed powerful language that succinctly explained the rationale for redefining the high school experience. Phrases and slogans like "overeating at a buffet," the "race to nowhere," and "Do we really want *U.S. News & World Report* dictating our values?" aptly described the college admissions rat race most parents and students were internalizing. Consider these key phrases: "being versus doing"; "the Golden Ticket versus the Golden Opportunity"; "be countercultural"; "lead like an icebreaker"; "shift the focus and change the story"; "instead of preparing the path we are preparing the child"; and their recently trademarked tagline "Strengthened by Faith. Prepared for Life." These sticky statements explained the need and rationale for redefining the culture at OLu.

◆ *Organize and invest in time to dialogue about your school's challenges and opportunities for a redefinition process.* One way OLu quickly built momentum for their redefinition process revolved around the many courageous conversations faculty members had with one another. From pause.com summer sessions to self-reflection exercises to faculty meetings to intentional and devoted PLC time, the OLu faculty asked hard questions, reflected, elaborated, discussed, argued, and challenged one another throughout the entire process. They were inspired and felt ownership in the revamp. Now, they cannot stop talking about ways to enhance and build momentum on their progress.

◆ *Develop a long game and short game in terms of setting goals, enacting action plans to reach those goals, and accomplishing them.* Sometimes you need quick wins or little wins to build momentum for change. Once they committed to the redefinition process, the leadership of OLu diligently implemented some seemingly small changes that actually made a big impact. For example, school started later. The graduation ceremony changed. They implemented World Council and ROAM. While OLu successfully completed or implemented some of these short-term goals, the reeducation of constituents and area grade schools, embedding more SEL and EQ into daily courses, and assessing the long-term impact of the redefinition experience will take more time. All key constituents, however, can already observe the fruit that is being produced by the redefinition movement because of the successful completion of several short-term goals.

◆ *Stay focused on God's Word and His mission for you and your school.* There is nothing more rejuvenating than to conduct a comprehensive review of your school and its mission with new eyes inspired by God's Word. OLu has been a terrific school, one of the best high schools in the country, for several decades. They could have rested on their bona fides and laurels; no one from the outside would have cared or dared to challenge OLu's outstanding reputation. God's Word, however, changes and moves people. You are either moving toward God or away from Him. If you are moving toward Him, He promises that He has great plans for you (Jeremiah 29:11). As Jesus says in Luke 12:48, "Everyone to whom much was given, of him much will be required, and from him to whom they entrusted much, they will demand the more." As a leader, ask and answer these questions each year: What is God calling us to do right now? How is He shaping or redefining our mission? How do we execute our mission?

Leaders like Moritz and Smith understand and realize that they must pay attention to two scorecards—the secular and the spiritual. They are quite aware that many families send their children to OLu because they know their child will receive a top-notch education and significantly increase the odds that their son or daughter will be admitted to a topflight university. At the end of the day, however, both Moritz and Smith hit their pillows each night and ask a simple question: Are we (OLu) serving God or are we serving man? And in the great Lutheran traditions of being countercultural, being cutting edge in the education field, and getting to the crux of the matter, they sleep well knowing that they and their team are doing everything in their power to provide a successful and Christ-centered high school experience. A fallen world should not define what success means or looks like. Instead, we turn to God's Word for inspiration—the Word that became flesh. Being successful means being faithful and designing a high school with a distinct and God-pleasing purpose. Jesus redefined the relationship between God and man when He went to the cross and rose from the tomb. Inspired by His lead, OLu moves forward in faith, shifting the focus for a nearsighted world and changing the story to the greatest and only story that really matters. Better than any graduation ceremony or diploma, students are "Strengthened by Faith" and "Prepared for Life."

"Settled between Two Rivers, Showing the Way to the Water of Life"

11

THE THREE-ROOM SCHOOLHOUSE:

TRINITY LUTHERAN SCHOOL ORCHARD FARM

ST. CHARLES, MO

The Challenge and Opportunity

"Settled between two rivers, showing the way to the water of life." That is the mission of Trinity Lutheran School Orchard Farm, a school that not only rests between two rivers but in some ways rests between two worlds, bridging the best of the past and the promising educational practices of the emerging future. In this final story of the book, we thought it proper to draw the reader's attention to the longest operating school in our list, located in a rural area outside of St. Charles, Missouri, since 1862. During this time, the school continues to faithfully serve a small population of students, with a K–8 enrollment never exceeding fifty in a given year. While not a one-room schoolhouse (it is, in fact, a three-classroom schoolhouse, but with some other very nice facilities alongside those classrooms), it embodies the best of such a tradition and remains firmly rooted in the time-tested practices and values of Lutheran education while also embracing some modern technologies and innovative teaching practices. It does this and more while being a tuition-free school for member families, apart from a modest registration fee.

THE TRINITY LUTHERAN ORCHARD FARM STORY

The story of Trinity Lutheran Orchard Farm School goes back to the middle of the Civil War, when the Lutheran families of the Point Prairie district sought the formation of a school to meet the educational needs of their children. They built a one-room schoolhouse that opened in 1862 and continues to serve a small number of families to this day. While the facilities have expanded significantly since those early years, some things remained the same. They still require weekly memory work from the Bible and Martin Luther's Small Catechism, religion classes are taught daily, children gather weekly for chapel, and each day begins with a devotion and song.

As in the early days, Trinity remains in a rural setting, but now it is also in driving distance to more populated communities. Yet that intimate and caring feel of a one-room schoolhouse is very much alive and well, only with a modern and technology-enhanced flavor, a fascinating blend of tradition and innovation.

Like the longstanding one-room-schoolhouse model, Trinity operates multigrade classrooms organized largely into upper and lower grades. In such a context, older students care for and help younger students. Student collaboration and cooperation is a commonplace and natural part of the environment. Furthermore, there is ample opportunity for individualized student work and customized learning based on the unique needs of each learner.

Unlike the schoolhouse of old, Trinity students are supported with a wealth of technologies. The entire school is Wi-Fi accessible and there is some sort of one-to-one program at work throughout the school (Chromebooks, tablets, and laptops, depending upon the grade or situation). Google Classroom is used in grades three through eight, creating a virtually paperless environment. There is a 3-D printer, Lego robotics kits, a computer for video editing, software for teaching computer programming and other skills, and a STEAM (science, technology, engineering, arts, and math) Lab that is well-suited for technology-enhanced project-based learning.

All of this happens with a school of forty-two students (two nonmember students) and a teaching staff of three, all of whom are graduates from one of the colleges in the Concordia University System. This small size allows for teachers to be flexible and creative in what and how they teach, while also getting to know each student personally, attending to the unique gifts, strengths, abilities, and challenges of each learner. If a learner comes with challenges that require additional assistance, the school has an ongoing partnership with the local public school for the necessary special education services.

This is a truly distinct school culture and context, calling for teachers with the right mix of gifts and an understanding of education in the Lutheran tradition. As such, experience tells them that called teachers or at least graduates from the Concordia University System seem to be an important part of the mix. This is a close-knit community, with teachers coming to know the intimate details about students and their families; approaching this role as a teaching ministry is an important part of the school culture.

While it is a small community, there is some racial diversity, not to mention children coming from a variety of different family contexts and backgrounds. Some of this is newer to the school. There was a time when almost every family lived and worked on farms, and a few families in the school still do. About half of the families are from the immediate Orchard Farms area, with others commuting from St. Charles or even farther away.

This school is tuition-free for member families, who make up almost the entire student body. This is thanks to the church seeing the school as a primary mission, funding the school with that in mind. The church's commitment to the school is a critical part of its ongoing success. For example, when a pastor recently retired after thirty years of ministry at the church and a search committee interviewed candidates to take his place, the second question for every candidate was, "How do you feel about Christian education?"

In a time when people often lift up and look to schools with a booming enrollment and massive facilities, the vibrant, stable, and faithful model of education embodied at Trinity Lutheran is an important reminder of yet another possibility for Lutheran education in the twenty-first century.

GOALS AND DESIRED OUTCOMES

The goal for Trinity from its Civil War days was to create a quality education for the children of the Lutheran families at the church, a goal rooted in a distinctly Lutheran mission and identity. That same goal persists after more than 150 years.

RESULTS AND OUTCOMES

As long as the congregation remains committed to the mission of the school, Trinity will continue to serve families well into the future. The supporting congregation has 700 people on the roster of baptized members and worships between 200 and 250 each Sunday. The church has no debt and is incredibly conservative with its finances. It typically refrains from any groundbreaking or new project until it is well on its way to raising the necessary funding. The budget to maintain the school and staff is secure, and the congregation remains committed to that important mission.

In terms of students, the school enrollment remains steady, with no real goal to grow beyond fifty students. Students go on to various high schools with a solid record of academic success. As described by one teacher, "Our graduates do really well."

This is a congregation with a love for the traditions of the Lutheran church and steady commitments over the years, including the commitment to this school. There is clearly great pride in this small gem of a Lutheran school and a persistent resolve to do what it takes to support it in the future. Perhaps that resolve is well represented by a comment from one of the teachers: "The school started in the Civil War. People of Missouri banded together to start this school in one of the most challenging times in our nation's history. This school is not going to end on my watch. Our church is a model of fierce dedication. Our congregation takes this to heart. This is a community of dogged determination. In the worst of times in our history, they said, 'We are going to start one of the best things in our community,' and they did it." The incredible pride and inspiration that comes from the longstanding vision and tradition associated with the school is alive and well today.

LESSONS FROM TRINITY LUTHERAN

Lessons about Lutheran education come from small and large schools alike, and there are plenty of valuable lessons for us to consider in this concluding story in the book. Consider just five of them before we venture into a summary list of lessons in the conclusion.

Multigrade Is a Method, Not Just a Necessity

Some people look at a school like this and assume that the multigrade classroom is just a matter of necessity due to limited teachers or small enrollment numbers. That is a reality, but there is also ample research to show the value and benefits of multigrade and multiage learning environments. Even in larger schools, this is a model worth exploring. At minimum, there is much that we can learn about it. In reality, the idea of dividing students into very discrete grades by narrow age brackets is a newer practice, and there is little to no evidence that this is the best or most effective way of teaching and learning. As such, a school like Trinity is a good reminder to imagine the possibilities for how we segment learners and learning.

Even Small Diamonds Are Valuable

If there is a solid and viable financial model, who is to say that a Lutheran school must be in the constant pursuit of massive growth? While we can celebrate and be inspired by schools bursting at the seams and achieving enrollments in the thousands, schools like this remind us that small learning communities can be strong, viable, and transformational for the students and families. There is ample room in the larger Lutheran education system for both. The idea that you need a larger number of students to be viable is often shaped by a tuition-dependent model or other business concepts about the economy of scale. There are indeed benefits to larger enrollments, but there are also important lessons and benefits to smaller and intimate learning communities as well. Some of our nation's great leaders, scientists, inventors, business people, church workers, and others benefited from an education resembling the one-room-schoolhouse model. It can be quite effective.

In fact, the idea of microschools is a new trend in contemporary education communities. Many people are tapping into the world of educational technology for more personalized and individualized instruction, combined with intimate and highly collaborative microlearning communities. In fact, there is a trend toward the launch of these small schools all over the country, each with their own distinctions. In fact, while researching this school, I couldn't help but think about the possibility of a national Lutheran management organization (not unlike Open Sky Education in chapter 9) that could be created to help grow, launch, and sustain these small but mighty schools around the country or even the world. There are many promising possibilities for us to consider in this regard.

Tradition Is a Powerful Tool for Missional Focus and Resolve

It is inspiring to hear the story of a school with such a long history, one that was born amid some of the darker or more challenging times in US history.

The Lutheran families resolved to have a school for their children, and they made it happen. That resolve has persisted for over 150 years on a small scale. Such missional focus and resolve is a source of inspiration for many of us in Lutheran education today.

We Can Blend Tradition and Innovation in Lutheran Education

Trinity is a wonderful model of taking the best of the past and blending it with promising and emerging practices. They hold firm to Lutheran catechesis; rituals and practices around worship and religious instruction throughout the week; and the importance of memory work. They have traditional subjects and approaches to teaching as well. They also engage students with project-based learning, inquiry-based learning, rich field trips, technology-rich STEAM activities, and more.

Imagine the Possibilities

The purpose of this book is to help us imagine the breadth of possibilities for Lutheran education, considering the affordances and limitations of each, seeking lessons and takeaways that have relevance for your current context or perhaps a future one. If we are going to truly imagine the possibilities, then it is helpful to look into our past and to consider possible futures. It is with that in mind that this final story of Trinity Lutheran Orchard Farm School is a perfect concluding story. It draws us into and reminds us of a past that has fascinating relevance for the current times, but it also shows how a long-standing school remains constant in important ways while innovating and experimenting in others.

In the following conclusion, we have drawn together themes and threads from the many stories in this book to offer twenty-five concluding ideas as you join us in imagining the possibilities for Lutheran education now and in the future.

Conclusion

25 LESSONS LEARNED

There is so much that we learned through our study of these schools. Sometimes they were lessons shared directly from those we observed and interviewed or through the school documents and websites we read and reread. In other cases, these lessons grew from our own reflection, prompted by these schools' compelling, creative, and even courageous choices. We learned from successes and failures, from what people shared and sometimes from what people did not share. In fact, we suspect that you as the reader experienced the same thing as you read and reflected on these different stories. You undoubtedly have a long list of thoughts, questions, and lessons.

While our list of lessons could be long enough to warrant a separate book, we condensed that list to twenty-five lessons learned from these stories, these case studies of thriving Lutheran schools. These are lessons that emerged from several, or sometimes almost all of the cases, representing important themes that spanned the wide array of schools in this book and the contexts in which they thrive. We are convinced that these twenty-five lessons present sage advice for any Lutheran school and anyone who is open and committed to imagining the possibilities for Lutheran education.

We do not presume that all the lessons will be earth-shattering surprises. Some will appear new to readers; others will affirm the reader's own thoughts and experiences. Regardless, they are noteworthy, valuable guides as each of us consider how we can promote a growing, thriving, faithful ecosystem of Lutheran schools around the world.

1. Lutheran schools will succeed, and they will fail.

Even as we told the stories of these seemingly thriving Lutheran schools, many of them faced significant challenges along the way. They have more challenges in their future. In some cases, these schools have significant debt to overcome. Others must navigate complex policy and regulatory landscapes that could change quickly, leaving the school to reinvent its financial model and approach to educational ministry. Demographic changes are always at work, not to mention how the economy affects the ability of some to afford or choose a Lutheran school. These real challenges come from inside and out, and there is no guaranteed success.

There will always be risks, but it is not necessarily a character flaw to fail in an endeavor. That is part of trying something uncertain and challenging. This is nothing new to God's people. Yet we persist because we know that while failure is possible in some areas, it is not in the most important areas. God will *not* fail us. He is faithful and keeps His promises. He will never leave or forsake us. These are the foundations of the Christian life. They do not guarantee success, but they do provide a foundation from which we have the courage and perspective to take calculated risks, to move forward.

2. Do not settle for survival.

Excellence does not emerge by chance. It comes from careful thinking, planning, and acting. It calls for clarity, conviction, and accountability. This is consistently demonstrated in the schools that we profiled. These are stories of incredibly hard work, the pursuit of good and right thinking, and the drive to pursue a distinct approach to education that is also distinctly Lutheran in its mission. These school leaders study the context and seek input from others on how best to respond. Then, as they go about their work, they are constantly seeking feedback and providing it to others, all focused on the goals and vision of the school.

In doing so, they move from a mind-set of surviving, just trying to keep the school doors open, to truly thriving. This does not mean that they fail to struggle with very real challenges that could one day lead to problems or even the risk of closing. However, there is a compelling and clear standard for excellence and a constant and steady set of actions toward meeting and exceeding that standard. Without that, it is too easy to fall into complacency and even a simple survival mode.

3. Do not be generic.

The world and the local community do not need just another school. They need great schools with a distinguishable identity. People inside the community should be able to articulate what is distinguishable, and a school's communication to those outside of the school should reflect that as well. In most communities and contexts, families have countless options for education. What makes this school worth consideration? This cannot be just a marketing task. It starts with actually becoming that difference in the school. Just as God created only one of you in all of history, your school was also created to be one of a kind. Embrace your God-given brand. Promoting something that you cannot deliver lacks honesty and integrity. Every school profiled in this book is far from generic. It has one or a few clearly distinguishable traits, and it is not hard for people to see them in action.

4. Do not compete; differentiate.

Sometimes we see the nearby school as our competition, and we adjust our offerings in direct response to that competition. Interestingly, while this competition mind-set was present for the schools in this book, it did not drive or dominate. Instead, the schools started with a compelling vision for their own school. It was more about who they are, whom they want to serve, and how they want to serve. Additionally, the focus was on prospective families, how best to connect with them, and how to provide something of value to them instead of how to compete for students with another school.

There is the obvious reality that families have and make choices, and that is sometimes a factor worth considering, but for the thriving school, it does not wait to change until the "competition" forces the issue. They are driven by a mission and vision that moves them to grow, improve, and deepen the quality of what they are doing.

5. Do not settle for Lutheran icing on a public education cake.

"Do what the public schools do, but then add Jesus to it." That was not the slogan of any school in this book. Of course, few to no Lutheran schools explicitly state such a thing as their plan. Yet, in practice, that is a temptation for some schools. We look to what these schools are doing, replicate it, and then add our distinctly Lutheran elements to it. The public school system often sets the agenda for what constitutes school, and people start from that foundation. Yet a careful look at many of the schools profiled in this book tells a different story. These are schools that build their foundations on what is most important to them and develop values in their unique context. They deal with regulatory and compliance matters as much as any other school, but that is not the starting point.

6. Establish a clear, compelling vision and philosophy for your school.

The ability to clearly articulate a vision and distinctiveness is perhaps one of the most important lessons of this book. Without a clear vision and wholehearted commitment to that vision, schools struggle, even if they have their finances in order and adequate enrollment. The story of Immanuel Lutheran School is perhaps one of the most striking examples of this, but many other stories show something similar. In fact, when you walk the halls of some of these schools, you literally see the vision and philosophy on the walls of hallways and classrooms. It is part of the community's common vocabulary, their rituals, the policies and procedures, and of course the curriculum. While the staff may have different viewpoints on some matters, thriving schools tend to have school-wide core elements to the vision and philosophy. In fact, embedding the vision into a school is so important that it warrants a separate lesson of its own.

7. Create rituals, policies, and practices that draw everyone deeper into the vision and philosophy.

As a school leader, you are the caretaker of the vision and philosophy of the school. So ask these important follow-up questions: How do people know that vision and philosophy? How do new and prospective family members learn about it? How do new faculty learn about it? How do you make sure that it is front of mind for long-standing faculty and staff? How do the policies in the school muzzle or amplify the vision and philosophy? What do you do when you discover that a practice or policy is unexpectedly deviating from the vision and philosophy? How does the language used in the school point people back to the vision and philosophy? What daily and weekly rituals draw people to the vision and philosophy? In other words, it is not enough to write down the vision as some sort of exercise. The schools in this book have answers to many, sometimes all, of these questions. They are intentional and relentless about making the vision and philosophy real in the community.

8. Embrace continuous improvement.

None of the schools in this book have reached a final destination where they are content simply maintaining what they are doing right now. While maintaining what they are doing well is a priority, every one of these schools also presented leaders who look ahead to what is next or continually seek to improve what they are doing. They all recognize that their efforts are a continual work in progress. This is part of the Lutheran heritage. Martin Luther was not the first to call for reformation. However, his use of new technology—the printing press—allowed his interpretations and reflections on Scripture to spread. His thoughts and writings literally went global and, by God's grace, changed the world.

9. Embrace humble conviction.

It is inspiring to speak with the leaders and team members of thriving Lutheran schools. They consistently speak with confidence and conviction. Not all of these people are charismatic extroverts; they span personality types. Yet they share a confidence and conviction about key aspects of what they are doing. At the same time, it does not come off as arrogance or thinking that they have everything figured out. Instead it can be described as a sort of humble conviction. They have a core set of ideas to which they hold firm, but at the same time, they are open to correction, feedback, and learning. In fact, the culture of learning in these schools permeates leadership—places where not only students but teachers and leaders seek to grow and learn as well. As we all know, the humility to admit what we do not know and to learn from others is an important disposition for learning, and it is commonplace among the leaders and many others in schools featured in this book.

10. Do not underestimate the importance of a leader with vision and determination.

Especially in this contemporary age, people love the idea of grassroots efforts, flat organizational charts, and collaborative approaches to work. But as we heard these schools' stories of birth, rebirth, and growth, most had a strong leader with a vision and determination to see through the movement, change effort, or make the vision a reality. In the end, there must be a person or core group of people who hold up the vision and persist toward the desired goals for the school. Leadership matters.

11. Build a willing coalition.

While a strong, determined, and visionary leader is important for the success of these schools, none of these schools grew into thriving learning communities because of just one person. Schools intentionally built a willing and committed coalition. Often this involved drawing the support and engagement of board members, congregational members, current teachers, current parents and students, key community partners, financial partners, and others.

This typically involved building a strong and growing internal coalition—building a team around a shared vision and set of goals. It also frequently involved seeking out key partnerships with experts and people who had important knowledge or resources needed to be successful. This is a valuable lesson for other schools to carefully assess who the key stakeholders are (both internally and externally) and how to invite and involve them.

12. Recognize that money matters, and it reflects values.

None of these schools are money stories, but money plays a role in operating a sound and viable school. As seen in this book, there are many possibilities for funding a school. Within the stories of this text, we see incredible financial support from congregational members, funding significant building projects and even covering the tuition. We see others who obtained government funding. Others creatively leveraged rental fees to fund ministry. Then there are tuition-dependent schools, partnerships with charitable organizations, and more. There are many ways to fund a Lutheran school, but each of these schools carefully considered the options and selected a strategy that worked best in their context.

Similarly, when you look at how these schools spend their money, you see that the line items of a school budget are not just about money. They are powerful indicators of beliefs and priorities. Schools invest their time and resources in what is most important to them. While some are uncomfortable thinking and talking about money in a school ministry context, it is an important part of the plan. In fact, due diligence in this area is part of what makes it possible to think less about the money and more about the educational goals and purpose of the school.

One other observation on the Lutheran school funding issue: it has not escaped our attention that urban schools with vouchers and suburban schools in affluent zip codes seem to be healthier financially than, perhaps, some more traditional middle-class schools that are experiencing church membership stagnation or decline and other changing demographic forces. This trend only accentuates the point that Lutheran schools must constantly be thinking of creative and innovative ways to fund their schools in the future. Margins matter.

13. Crave feedback.

Some fear feedback because they worry what it will say about them or their work. They might consider negative feedback to be an indictment. Yet feedback is what allows us to identify problems, to grow, and to improve. Review the stories in this book and you will see a common trend of school cultures where leaders seek feedback, teachers seek and receive feedback about their teaching, and students learn to value feedback as well.

14. Learn and adjust.

It is not just feedback for the sake of getting feedback. Feedback helps us figure out what is working and what is not. This is a disposition of leaders and teachers who care about excellence and the quality of what they are doing. Some want the perception of doing well. Others are in the pursuit of actual, objective excellence; that is what we repeatedly observed in these schools. These communities value feedback and know how to use it to learn and adjust what they are doing to better align with their values and goals. Moreover, in the twenty-first century, when people can change the direction of an endeavor with a quick click, Lutheran schools must make their adjustments quicker. There is a saying in sports that speed kills. In the education world today, a slow reaction may kill your school instead. When it comes to responding positively to feedback, do as legendary basketball coach John Wooden once said: "Be quick, but don't hurry."

15. Prepare for and persist through inevitable setbacks.

When you revisit the stories in this book, you find that none of them are without setbacks, sometimes significant ones. Some actually grew out of past failures, regrouping, and moving forward into better times. Some launched only to find early challenges that left their future uncertain. Others faced steady and frequent challenges along the way and worked through them prayerfully and deliberately. Still others operate in such fluid and challenging contexts that every day seems like working through setbacks in one area while making progress in another. This is, of course, the nature of life in a fallen world, but it is also especially representative of the good and important work of contemporary Lutheran education. Facing such setbacks can be discouraging. It is important and useful to recognize that the challenges and setbacks are part of the work, sometimes even the part that creates the greatest and most promising opportunities.

16. Make teacher accountability and equipping a top priority.

A school cannot remain faithful to its mission and core philosophy without a teaching staff who embrace that mission and philosophy, have the knowledge and skill to enact it in practical ways, receive the support and accountability to keep focused on what is most important, and are constantly learning and deepening their core commitments. The schools in this book assured teacher commitment to the mission in different ways, but the resolve in this area was a constant. These schools are diligent about finding the right teachers for the task at hand, making sure that they are well equipped and supported toward specific goals, holding them accountable, and building a community where the teachers uphold the mission and support one another in doing so. The schools in this book that maintain high quality academics and mission integrity make this a top priority. They have specific plans, rituals, budgets, and often even dedicated personnel to make this a top priority. They do not leave this to chance or assume that simply hiring the "right people" is enough. This is an ongoing focus for schools of excellence.

17. Grow something beautiful in the fertilized soil of failure.

This list of twenty-five lessons already included two lessons about failures and setbacks. This is a third because it speaks to the origin of many schools.

Many of these school stories started in early narratives about failure. In some of the stories, you read about vacant school buildings, declining enrollments, diminishing focus on mission and Lutheran identity, and more. There are countless stories not told in this book that ended in such a way. These are different stories because some of them are, in a way, resurrection stories. By God's grace, we learn from these stories that new life, new focus, and new opportunities emerged out of less-than-pleasant circumstances. We pray that some readers will find hope in this fact, that they will look at what might seem to be a story of impending failure in a local Lutheran school, revisit it, and discover that it might not be the end of the story but actually the beginning of an exciting journey into new ministry opportunities, a refocus on and reaffirmation of Lutheran mission and identity, or an invitation to reach and serve new people in new ways.

18. Expect great days ahead.

One of the joys that comes from working on a book like this, visiting schools and interviewing leaders in Lutheran education, is that it is a lesson in hope and encouragement. There are so many gifted leaders in Lutheran education who are part of incredibly inspiring Lutheran education stories. To read these stories is to be encouraged about the future of Lutheran education. It is our hope and prayer that you, as a reader, experienced something similar. The story of Lutheran education is not one of declining enrollments, financial struggles, stagnation, subpar academics, and struggles to maintain a mission-focused identity. That is a reality for some today, but when we look at the larger story of Lutheran education, we are convinced that the types of stories in this book point us to a real and viable future. We invite you to join us in helping to make that a reality.

19. Continue to imagine the possibilities.

The title of this book is *Imagine the Possibilities* for a good reason. It is easy for us to see only our immediate Lutheran education context and miss what is happening in the larger system. We can find ourselves so consumed by the daily tasks and challenges that we do not consider the many other possibilities. One simple but important lesson in this book is that, regardless of what is happening at your school, there are more possibilities to consider, and those possibilities might just be what is needed in your school, church, or community.

It is our hope that you will draw from individual stories and pull different pieces from various stories to get you thinking about promising possibilities. As co-authors of this book, we admit that it would be a delight to meet a reader of this book at a conference and hear inspiring stories of how something from this book inspired or instigated a brand-new story, one equally worthy of highlighting in a book of promising practices in Lutheran education. Perhaps someone will read about the classical Lutheran school, combine that with the idea of a charter school management organization for scaling efforts, and create a similar entity that allows the replication and scaling to dozens of new and high-quality classical Lutheran schools around the world. Maybe another will be moved by the idea of a tuition-free school for member and nonmember families, combine that with the idea of online learning, and come up with a means of reaching thousands of new families. Or perhaps you can tell us how your school merged or created a network with other area Christian schools to maximize resources and connections. Those are only a couple of ideas, but the readers of this book will collectively have hundreds or thousands of their own. This is the imagining of the possibilities, in many ways.

20. Always seek mission-driven decisions and innovation.

Another valuable aspect of this book is that none of the stories are about trends and fad-chasing efforts in contemporary education. These are not stories about new educational bells and whistles, although some of the schools do indeed use state-of-the-art technology. These are often meticulously researched, carefully considered, prayerfully pursued endeavors. They are shaped by mission-driven decisions and innovation. In other words, each choice and step in the process is tested to ensure it furthers the core mission of the organization. This sort of mission-sifting is not only important but also essential for a school of distinction and excellence to maintain a firm commitment to the historic mission so central to Lutheran education.

The leaders and many others in these schools know what they are doing, but they also have a deep understanding about why they are doing it. The why for decisions is embedded in the culture because these communities think and care deeply about their mission and core beliefs.

21. Have the courage and conviction to say no to some ideas.

A mission-minded approach to decisions and innovation is not just about what you do. It is also what you choose not to do. As seen throughout this book, choosing excellence in one area is often about prioritizing time, money, and effort in one direction and not another. It is about saying no to some things in order to say yes to others.

22. Listen to and learn from the community.

The schools profiled in this book consistently grounded themselves in their mission and core beliefs but also in their specific community and context. What does it look like for us to live out our mission, philosophy, and core beliefs in our context? What are the needs of the people in this community? How can we best communicate and connect with the people in the community, especially prospective families? What is our role in the community? Having a clear mission and Lutheran identity did not drive them into some isolationist endeavor. Instead, it inspired them to look beyond their school to the community. By listening to people in the community and learning from what they heard, they were better positioned to respond. This is not listening and learning to compromise, but to better understand their distinct role and contribution to that community. Think of this as an important and ongoing organizational self-awareness that helps the school to respond, adapt, and communicate in ways that are important to the school's ongoing success.

23. Abandon the myth of lone ranger Lutheran education.

People are building connections and affiliations in this digital age in ways unlike any time in history. Arguably, Lutheran educators are still figuring out the implications for strong connections, collaborations, and affiliations. While there are growing and important exceptions to this, Lutheran schools are largely isolated from one another. Yet the stories in this book show that many consultants, resources, connections, collaborations, and affiliations helped each school in its journey.

This is a powerful lesson and source of inspiration for what is possible. We are only beginning to wake up to what this could mean for extending the mission and ministry of Lutheran education. It is a lesson worth noting—one that thriving schools are figuring out faster than others. They are learning to network based on a shared vision and philosophy instead of getting together for coffee with the school down the road (not that this is a bad idea). In doing so, they are discovering the power of networking and collaborating in ways that may be a key to serving new families, reinvigorating struggling schools, and launching new ones. We invite readers to join in helping Lutheran education as a whole embrace the power of networked educational ministry on a global scale.

24. Prepare for succession; build a legacy.

As inspired as we are by the stories in this book, it is also important to recognize that the future for these schools is still uncertain. In fact, as authors of this text, we confess the fear of choosing to profile a thriving school that, soon after publication of the book, takes a turn for the worse. Funding falls through. Internal challenges undermine the efforts. Unexpected external pressures slow, halt, or diminish the positive movement. Perhaps changes in high-level personnel result in schools losing sight of their mission and philosophy, gradually or suddenly hindering the prior successes. These are all potential futures. As we already recognized, the work of Lutheran education always brings with it some measure of risk and uncertainty.

Yet there are some ways that we can strive to avoid such future possibilities, especially when it comes to succession planning. We met and learned about many great, inspiring, and effective leaders in the course of studying these schools, and they will not be at these schools forever. That is why it is important that these schools are not built around a single person or personality but around a mission, a vision, and core values that are shared widely across the community and increasingly embedded in the school culture. It is also why leaders of such schools are wise to think about strategic delegation of tasks over time, intentionally mentoring others and essentially thinking of working themselves out of a job. Such prayerful and deliberate work is a wise and important part of building a school of excellence for the long-term.

25. A final challenge: consider the possibility of the next great Lutheran school.

This brings us to the final lesson and concluding comments for this book. This last one is a challenge more than it is a lesson. In fact, it is both a prayer and a dream for us as the authors. Our writing this book has been a source of rich personal growth and learning about Lutheran education. Yet we also see this as a gift to the church. It is a gift that we pray will be supremely useful. Even more, our dream is that it will inspire the current and next generation of leaders in Lutheran education to imagine the possibilities and, having done so, take what they learn to help revitalize struggling schools, expand the mission and ministry of others, and even to launch a whole new set of Lutheran schools that serve families and students in the United States and around the world. In essence, it is our hope and prayer that you as the reader will help to create the next great story of Lutheran education and, in doing so, share the love of God in Jesus Christ broadly as we equip students in mind, body, and spirit for service to Jesus Christ in the church and the world.

DISCUSSION GUIDE

The following questions are meant to be used after each chapter in a flexible manner by groups or individuals reading this text. As the title suggests, we hope that each case study inspires innovative thoughts and creative ideas that you may want to implement at your own organization.

1. *The school you just read about had a specific story or background that inspired leaders to develop a particular educational approach or concept. Use these questions to reflect on your own school or organization: What's your compelling story? Is the story changing? Does it need to change? Does everybody know the story? What is the new story your school or organization needs to write or embrace? Why?*

2. *Almost every Christian school faces several challenges or obstacles in their ongoing ministry. In this particular case study, however, we focused on a specific challenge, or set of challenges, that the school had to confront. Before you can come up with a solution to anything, you must know the problem. Think about your own school or organization: What is your holy discontent? What is the compelling challenge or obstacle inhibiting the growth, development, or advancement of your ministry?*

3. *Throughout this case study, analogies, metaphors, images, Scripture passages, and comparisons were used to capture the essence of the mission or the compelling reason to implement a unique educational approach. What are some powerful or compelling analogies, metaphors, images, Scripture passages, and comparisons that currently identify and articulate your mission or unique educational approach? What are some that could be articulated to drive a new educational approach or mission?*

4. This case study shared lessons for Christian leaders and schools. After reading this case study, what two or three concepts, ideas, initiatives, or lessons impressed you the most? Why? How could you apply any of them to your context?

5. As you read the case study, you probably had many questions or "want to know more" moments. We encourage you to reach out to the leaders of these schools to ask your questions directly if you are so moved. For the moment, identify which questions about the case study rise to the top of your curiosity list. What do you want to learn more about?

6. After reading about this particular school, write down as many brainstorming ideas as you can. Do not take time to judge the validity of your ideas or possibilities—just write them down to ponder and pray about. Run your brainstorm possibilities and ideas by colleagues and professionals. Once you have imagined several possibilities for your school, narrow your list and identify three possibilities that you feel most excited about and compelled to bring to fruition for your school or organization. What are your top three ideas or possibilities that you want to become realities in your school or organization?